CASE IN POINT

Investigating Private Investigations

MR. JOHN C. BILYK JR

ISBN: 0692025820
ISBN 13: 9780692025826

CONTENTS

FALSE IMPRESSIONS

The impression someone gets when you say that you are a private investigator (PI) is that you were once a law enforcement officer (LEO) or had some law enforcement background. While this may have been true in the past, the modern-day PI has been in this profession his or her entire career.

As I was growing up, there were many PI shows on TV. Private-investigator or private-detective shows were a hit in the 1980's and 90s. Shows like *Simon and Simon*, *The Rockford Files*, and *Magnum PI* were some of the more popular ones. Today, we are intrigued by more scientific-content shows like *CSI* and *Numbers*.

I knew when I was in high school that I wanted to be an investigator. Although I was never the best student, I could communicate well with others and got along with many different types of people. I learned my strong work ethic not from studying but through my persistence in athletics. I excelled in sports and eventually played college football. If it hadn't been for football, I'm not sure what my alternatives might have been. I know I thought casually about joining the military, but at eighteen years old, I wasn't serious about anything and didn't plan more than a week in advance. I don't even recall ever having even filled out a college application. After high school I was recruited, along with three of my other teammates. For me it was entrance into college, and although they didn't have a criminal justice program, I settled on psychology. With an Italian family business at home, the elders in my family assumed that I would eventually come home and be a butcher. Our family business dated back to my grandfather's immigration to the United States through Ellis Island in the early 1900s. My Sicilian grandfather pushed a fresh fish cart around the streets of a small steel mill town west of Philadelphia, called Phoenixville. He eventually went on to raise pigs and cattle, build a slaughterhouse, and sell fresh-cut meat in a retail market on Church Street. My grandfather John passed away while my mother was still in high school. The original butcher shop on Church Street was taken over by my great-uncle and my mother's brother Jack. My uncle Jack would later branch out on his own and build the family's second business location on Pothouse Road. This store continues today and is still a family-run market.

After my first football season, I suffered a knee injury and started to think about the depth of my wish to continue the sport. I was also feeling the pressure from my family to work in the family business. My older cousin Scott had already joined his father, and I was the next oldest boy expected to join my great-uncle. I researched a local university about forty-five minutes away and found that they had a criminal justice program. I figured I could continue learning the meat business and chase my goals of being an investigator at the same time. For the next three years, I went to night school, eventually completing my BS in the administration of criminal justice (CJ). Among the core courses in policing, evidence, corrections, probation, and parole, I heard nothing about the field of private investigations as a career. It wasn't until my senior year in college when a professor invited a private investigator into the classroom to speak about the subject and how I could go from college directly into an investigations field.

Like many CJ majors, I had my sights on being a federal agent, working with the FBI, DEA, or US Customs. As I now see it, there are just many more talented people then there are entry-level jobs available to students directly out of college. My passion for a challenging investigative career was about to take a turn toward a new growing industry, offering so many different and diverse opportunities. This industry would, however, not be with the government; it would be in the private sector.

I recall when I was in college and attended a criminal justice career exposition; the information circulating was that many of the federal law-enforcement positions were for people in other disciplines. The "feds" wanted graduates in the sciences: computer, chemistry, and biology. The federal government needed agents familiar with Internet technology, chemical, and biohazards for more science-intensive forensic investigations. It seemed clear to me that they needed specialists in technical areas of study—not someone trained in the social sciences of criminal justice, its historical evolution, the administration, or psychology of the criminal mind. It's no secret that many CJ majors come from athletic pools, where their brains and brawn overcome a lack of experience to make them suitable for the front lines of local law enforcement agencies. With thousands of CJ majors graduating each year, many qualified candidates find themselves going into the many jobs that policing offers. But those coveted federal investigative jobs are more difficult to land. They are also less prevalent as many federal investigation positions are filled by law enforcement officers (LEOs) who had a couple of years of proven experience or even law degrees. There are also many talented candidates coming from the investigative branches of the Armed Services. The army's criminal investigations division (CID) and counterintelligence corps (CIC) discharge many qualified candidates. So competition for the typical CJ graduate looking to land a federal investigations position comes with stiff competition. Competition from other majors outside the CJ discipline with science backgrounds, LEOs with some proven experience, and the Armed Services, whose applicants often had more general investigations experience than most local police department LEOs.

So the typical CJ major may find that his or her path to land that federal investigative position will entail stiff competition and most likely warrant some degree of proven work experience.

The private investigator speaking in my college classroom opened another alternative for me. By my senior year, I had already worked a part-time position at a Maryland shore police department. I couldn't see myself as a police officer and knew I was different from most of the other career officers I worked alongside during the summer. I had that entrepreneurial spirit best described as wanting a true challenge and being paid well for my effort. I didn't think I was going to get that by remaining to be a police officer, nor did I want to put in the time that I thought it would take to be promoted into the investigative ranks of the department.

While I may have been only twenty-one years old, my gut feeling that policing wasn't for me couldn't have been more correct. Looking back, my personality and motivation to be a professional businessperson and make money was a distinguishing reason. I just didn't have the same chemistry that makes a good police officer. In the same regard though, I never wanted to be a police officer; I wanted to be an investigator. If you ask any officer how he or she spends most of his or her time, the officer will usually tell you that it is consumed by motor-vehicle-related stops. Police also routinely find themselves circulating in high crime areas and dealing with lower-economic-related disputes and crimes. They have difficult jobs, never knowing what to expect and always needing to be on guard. They are trained to take control of a situation, but they seem to have difficulty turning off their authoritarian poise. While these traits may be helpful to them in the field, they are not regarded characteristics to the professional private investigator or to the corporate industry we serve. Having been a hiring manager for a large private investigations firm, I can tell you that I usually approached hiring police officers with reservations. I found that this same reservation about hiring law enforcement officers rang true with many of my counterparts in other large agencies across the country. The time a candidate spent as a police officer usually determined the effect it had on his or her application. What motivates a person to become a police officer is different from what motivates a person to want to go into private investigative work. I recently interviewed the president of the investigations division of a large corporate firm with roughly 460 nationwide staff investigators. Ironically, I had hired him out of college nearly two decades earlier and had employed him as a staff investigator. Now running the investigative division of a large publicly traded company, he stated that in his company, the percentage of investigators with law enforcement backgrounds is less than 10 percent and probably closer to 5 percent.

The field of private investigations seemed better suited for the entrepreneurial-spirited person, looking for a challenging work environment where he or she was paid based on performance. Our industry distinguishes itself in many ways by the people who make up our industry, what we do, and how we do it. In contrast to the high visibility of police in their effort to deter crime, private investigators are trained to keep a low profile, hopefully entering a neighborhood and exiting it without anyone ever knowing they were there. We spend many hours conducting research and writing thorough and detailed reports. In addition, there are risks we undertake daily, and they start at the onset of our initial assignment. We need to be able to get the results our clients need, and many times this means taking on personal risks.

During a mobile tail, the target may get a jump on us, and we have the choice to let him or her go and come back another day or push the speed limit to try and catch up to them. Another subject may live in a gated community, and the only way you can possibly do your job is to get inside. These are just two examples of situations that we routinely face, and we need to do our job, knowing that we have no special privileges protecting us from getting a speeding ticket or being cited for trespass. It seems ironic that, while investigating a potential insurance-fraud felon, I have to put myself at risk while doing so. But risks are always part of the investigator's equation, and the risks we take as private investigators are far less risky than, let's say, an undercover drug-enforcement agent. While we may risk a ticket or, most likely, a verbal lashing, there are investigators risking their lives that are no different from us but who have so much more on the line.

As private investigators we are always expected to be professionals as we usually represent large corporations, attorneys, and insurance companies. These industries have an evolved sense of expectation when it comes to the professionalism of their workers and the company's reputation. Many industries invest heavily in their workers' training to keep their skill sets up-to-date. They expect us, as contractors, to uphold these same standards. Skills such as self-management, creativity, flexibility, and the ability to communicate your thoughts and ideas are just some of the necessary skills.

PIs are expected to be creative and resourceful in deciding how to approach a case and get the most favorable results. We must manage our time to be as productive and profitable in an industry known for thin margins and high expectations. To work within the corporate market, we must perform with similar standards of professionalism. I believe that having a small-business background made me a better employee for the investigative firm I went to work with. I already knew how important clients were and how easily they could just go shop elsewhere. When I became a lead investigator, I used to tell my trainees that there are many great chefs and bakers who start up businesses, but most restaurant and bakeries fail. It's not because the owners are not talented at their trade but because they don't have any business experience. In the private investigations business, investigations are the product we sell, but first and foremost we are a small business, statistically calculated to fail.

In 1982, I joined a small detective agency during a period when the industry was just breaking out and becoming more professionalized and specialized. The agency's goal was to become a nationwide company, only servicing the insurance and insurance defense industry.

The reality of the PI business is that the industry is very segmented and specialized. Investigative agencies specialize in a subject matter that the business owner knows best or in which he or she has some interest. The vast number of PIs aren't working many murders or missing person's cases. Fortunately, these aren't the high-volume caseloads that enable a PI or a PI firm to stay in business. A case every couple of weeks may have suited the retired law-enforcement detective that didn't want to work a full-time job, but the present-day career-oriented PI expects to work a forty- to fifty-hour workweek, fifty-two weeks a year. This means that the freshman PI entering the field looking for employment will search out a company entrenched in a market that produces constant work to support a career.

Perhaps the most overwhelming concept in discussing becoming a PI is that the profession is so broad. There are many different types of professionals in the field, performing so many different kinds of work. And the industry lends itself to new specialty areas cropping up all the time, especially as technology advances. Some of these new areas consist of investigating computer-related issues, such as hacking and identity theft. More traditional services include investigating copyrighted and trademark infringements, providing support in criminal and civil cases, insurance claims investigations, fraud, child custody, protection cases, and relationship screening. PIs also provide executive, corporate, and celebrity protection, and conduct pre-employment verification and individual background profiles. And of course they are hired to investigate individuals to prove or disprove infidelity, like the cases featured on the popular television show *Cheaters*. But the possible work scenarios can vary according to the needs of the client or the background of the investigator, who may have a particular skill or technical knowledge.

Private investigators often work irregular hours because of the need to conduct surveillance or contact people who are not available during normal working hours. Early morning, evening, weekend, and holiday work is often routine. Many professionals take a particular skill or profession and market it to the public. For example, you may have a fireman who decides to use his or her experience and work for an insurance company to assist in determining the cause and origin of a fire and who may advertise as a fire and arson investigator. Another professional who may have spent twenty years with the Florida Highway Patrol (FHP) may want to offer services in accident reconstruction as an automobile accident investigator. Maybe a T-shirt silk-screen printing professional who can tell the difference between a high-quality, Disney-printed T-shirt and the lesser quality of a pirated knock-off may want to engage in investigative work, identifying counterfeited products, their origin, and distribution. Private investigators are licensed in most states across the country. The states focus in on the activity or service offered, not your specialty. In most states the statute regulating PIs defines their activity as any "investigation by a person or persons for the purpose of obtaining information." If you are engaged in the business of seeking out information for hire, then you are required to be licensed.

A recent 2013 survey in a PI industry magazine looked into classifying the most common areas of the private investigations business. The author's survey suggested that the industry is broken down into ten specialty groups. These groups of specialties were further ranked by their percentage of business in the surveyed investigative firms. The most common assignment was reported as background investigations, followed by civil investigations, surveillance, other, insurance, fraud, corporate investigations, accident reconstruction, domestic investigations, and infidelity.

It should not be surprising that background investigations lead the list of most popular assignments. It is an investigation that anyone with just about any background can learn and conduct. I would also point out that criminal defense investigations was not identified as a specialty group but was included in the "other" category with other less-often-sought assignments.

The most common types of investigations in the survey are supported by the corporate and insurance defense industries. The largest investigative agencies will conduct nearly all of the specialty group investigations routinely, except for domestic and infidelity cases. The large, professional investigative agency will be devoted to training its investigators to perform all of these specialties as they may be required as part of one single investigation. Only the "other" and "accident reconstruction" categories may require specialized training, but then again, it would depend on the background of the investigator. Most of the categories identified by the survey would be within the scope and expectation of the private investigator looking to establish a career in the private investigations industry. So, regardless of your experience or lack of it, your training would be designed to make you skillful in most specialty areas so that you are a fully rounded investigator with complementing skills in all areas. After all, being an investigator means that you are engaging in an effort to search out and examine or learn the facts about something unknown or perhaps complex. You can't adequately perform satisfactorily if you are lacking some important skills or knowledge. Making sure that you learn these skills will be the responsibility of your trainer and a constant effort of your manager.

While we may debate the skills needed to perform any one of the mentioned specialty areas of investigations, a nontechnical professional, aiming for a career in private investigations, needs to start with the understanding of four basic building blocks of investigative activities: *surveillance, locate procedures, database resources and records searches, and statement taking.* Building experience in these four areas will enable you to tackle many commonplace investigations in the private sector and build more experience while doing so.

Depending on the assignment, the private investigators will determine the method in which the above activities are used or reported. We use the same investigative activities over and over again for many different types of cases. We constantly rely on the enormous amount of information that can be gained quickly using a computer to educate ourselves about different topics. The computer is a huge teaching tool to investigators who need to learn a little about many different topics. The computer will be such a vital learning tool that it will play an important role in training you as an investigator. The information available on the web from private and public sources is growing constantly, with the ability to research just about any topic. You need to understand a subject matter before you can adequately investigate it, and the computer will support this educational process. It may not only be a subject matter that you research. You may need to investigate a person as part of your investigation.

Information such as a subject's prior arrest history, convictions, civil filings, telephone numbers, motor vehicle registrations, property transactions, associations, club memberships, photographs, or personal profiles and activities from social media are all accessible online. Social media can even help track or find people as they upload content to their Facebook or send out tweets. In 2009, five teens (called the "Hollywood Hills Bunch") used the Internet as their accomplice in tracking celebrities. The teens tracked the movements of stars, such as Lindsay Lohan and Paris Hilton, and then broke into their houses, making off with millions of dollars in stolen possessions in a spree that lasted almost a year.

The police reported that the teens scoured celebrity blogs and websites, looking for pictures of the celebrities' valuables. The teens then used the Internet to find where the stars lived and raided the homes while the celebrities were away. The operations the teens used to assist their criminal escapade are some of the same activities a PI utilizes when hired to locate or track regular individuals. The PI will also have other sources of information, which are not accessible to the public, such as credit report information, propriety database sources, and other time-saving specialized programs that "mine" information from both public and private sources. Because this information can be used to find and track people, it is often regulated by states and federal statutes as well as by safeguards put in place by the provider through vetted subscription applications and secure access. It is not unusual to perform these searches and obtain personal identifying information, such as a person's home address, date of birth, and social security number. All such information can be very sensitive if released to the wrong party. This same information, if improperly discarded or in the wrong hands, can be used to steal someone's identity or for a more sinister matter, such as finding a person who purposely doesn't want to be found and has court-ordered protection in place.

PI HISTORY

By the 1980s the PI industry was going through a major transition with corporate and insurance matters taking precedence over the typical cases that PIs were accustomed to handling. And in many instances, the detective was not as qualified to serve the interests of the corporate client. PI companies needed to be larger, cover greater regions, and be more specialized, with higher standards of professionalism. The corporate clients expected efficiencies that the old gumshoe—in many cases, a retired law enforcement officer (LEO)—didn't understand. Videotape evidence was being introduced, but the early cost of the first reel-to-reel home-use video camera system was just under $10,000.00. Just the cost of a facsimile machine in the early 1980s was about $1,000.00. Change was occurring everywhere as technology continued to impact the way one business interacted with another business. The PI no longer just worked for the public; he or she was being hired by big business—and more often than ever before. In particular, the insurance industry was becoming the largest contractor of investigative services nationwide. There are varying statistics on the actual number of PIs nationwide. In 2012, the US Bureau of Labor and Statistics estimated that there were thirty thousand private investigators nationwide. In 2014, the PI industry estimated this to be closer to sixty thousand nationwide. Both sources agree that most investigators work in "agencies." *Agency* refers to the company that the investigators worked for, like "detective agency." Although, I would argue that the use of "detective agency" is antiquated as the more popular term is "investigative agency" or "investigative firm." The word *detective* is associated with law enforcement and investigating criminal activity. A more precise term would be "private investigator" so that we avoid implying that the subjects or subject matter we are investigating are criminal in nature.

In Florida, the Department of Agriculture and Consumer Services (DOACS) regulates the private investigative industry. Private investigative agencies are licensed through the division of licensing, which also falls under the DOACS. To open a private investigative agency, the applicant must secure a "Class A" agency license. The investigators within the agency are licensed individually with "Class C" licenses. There are also "Class CC" licenses, for investigator apprentices, called "interns." A private investigator cannot work without being associated with an "A" agency. This structure is also similar to a real estate sales person who must work for a real estate broker. The real estate broker or private investigative agency is the brick-and-mortar location of the business. Within this "A" agency, there is a specified management structure. There will be a manager (a qualifying agent with significant experience), "C" licensed investigators to work in the field, and "CC" apprentices (interns), who are learning from the more seasoned "C." The Bureau of Labor and Statistics reports that one out of every 5 PIs are self-employed, which should dismiss the idea that most PIs are a guy sitting behind his desk in the dark with a London Fog hanging on the coat rack just inside the glass door that is embossed with "Private Eye." Most PIs work in agencies with few Sam Spade types. If the agencies are small, they will employ anywhere from five to twenty investigators, with a combination of experienced licensed investigators and interns learning the business. Each "Class C" private investigator can train or apprentice up to six "Class CC" interns.

Larger national and international private investigative agencies will employ hundreds or more US private investigators. The investigators will be licensed and residents of each state where they work, and some states will have between ten and twenty investigators. In 2012, the Florida Division of Licensing reported that there were 8,034 "Class C" private investigators and 1,562 "Class CC" interns. They also reported 2,992 "Class A" private investigative agency licenses. With nearly three thousand agencies just in Florida, that's about forty agencies per county!

A PI's territory can consist of several counties, so in a seven-day workweek, he or she may find himself or herself on the road, traversing several cities before getting home for a rest and several days off. The larger agencies offer less travel as long as you are living in a metropolitan area. If you are an Orlando-based investigator with a large company, you could still expect to cover a seventy-five-mile radius to keep a full case load. The same company would also have investigators in Jacksonville to the north, Tampa to the west, Tallahassee and Pensacola to cover the Panhandle, and Miami to the south.

I embarked on my own PI history by packing my bags and moving to Fort Lauderdale, Florida. I had about five hundred dollars in cash when I arrived, and the first thing I did was buy a car at a "buy-here, pay-here" car dealer. I put the car purchase on my credit card to save what little cash I had. I ended up getting into a car accident, but I didn't have the money to have my car fixed. As a result it developed a broken engine mount, so every time I stepped on the gas, the engine would rise to one side, and the carburetor would flood out and stall the vehicle. In order for me to speed up the car, I would have to gingerly press on the gas pedal. Anyone considering doing surveillance would quickly realize that this car was not suited for the job. The damaged car looked so bad that when I parked it in a neighborhood to set up for surveillance, neighbors would call the police, thinking the car had been stolen, crashed, and abandoned.

Our PI agency specialized in conducting investigations for the insurance defense industry. It was the best field to be in because of the rising demand for insurance claim investigations. Insurance companies had staffed themselves with in-house investigators, but the amount of insurance fraud occurring was overwhelming. Insurance companies found that they could vend-out the work cheaper than continuing to add staff to keep up with the growing number of cases they wanted to have investigated.

I was trained to conduct background checks, locate investigations, conduct financial asset searches, conduct discreet neighborhood inquiries, take witness statements, and perform surveillance—elements of which I would use in all facets of the work I would do over the next thirty years. The sheer volume of work I would get from the insurance industry would challenge every skill I hoped to perfect and draw on my ability to search out information and knowledge. It also challenged my continued ability to be imaginative and resourceful. When you want to learn something about an organization, there is no better way than to infiltrate it. If shipments of products disappear on a loading dock or within a distribution center and you can go undercover, it doesn't usually take long to learn the details of what's going on. If you want to learn about a neighbor or a neighborhood, go into the area early in the morning, park your car, and watch. You would be surprised at what you can see and learn when no one knows you're watching.

But the PI business is also not just about how good we can be in the field. The reality of starting any business is that 70 percent of all new small businesses fail in the first three years, and 20 percent of those that make it through the first three years then fail within the next five years. A business that lasts ten years or more is, by all practicality, a successful establishment that will continue to thrive. In my thirty years of business, I have built two PI agencies, both of which exceeded sales of one million dollars and are still in business today. My practices and procedures are based on what I think are true and tested "best practices."

Throughout this book, I will relate cases where these principle practices and procedures were used successfully. What you won't read are the thousands of similar cases in which the same procedures were implemented and tested over and over again. You also won't read about criminal cases investigated and murders solved because that's not what most PIs do. A career PI works for corporate clients and investigates civil matters that may turn out to be criminal, but initially they had some business purpose that the corporate client needed to understand to prevent similar losses. As a career PI, I can more readily relate to the investigative journalist rather than to the stereotypical image of Sam Spade that you may get when you first hear that someone is a private investigator.

SURVEILLANCE

One of the most practical PI practices to learn is performing surveillance. If you can learn the do's and don'ts of successful surveillance, you will always have a skill or source of potential income. It's also a business that anyone of any age or gender can learn. But your success will depend on your ability to deliver results on a continuous basis. When I interview a surveillance investigator for a referral, I ask him or her if they get video on every case. If I hear a response that "it depends on if the target was active," I get suspicious of their ability. While this may sound like a practical response, it is also the response of the least successful. Surveillance is a science and not a job left for chance. Typically bad practices make the surveillance a game of chance; therefore, the least successful feel that their success rate depends on the chance that their subject is active. You can't successfully achieve consistent results relying on chance. Everyone is active to some degree. People have to shop; they have to eat, work, go to the bank, or even retrieve their mail. At some point you have to see your target. The real issue is whether

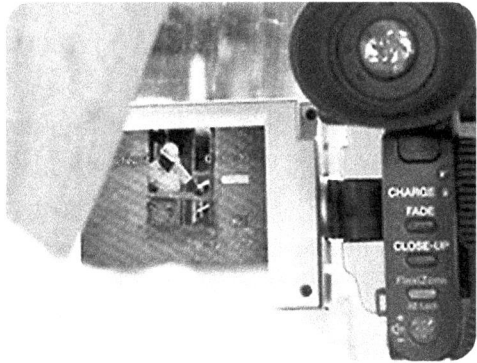

you are in the proper position to observe this activity or present at the right time of day. This is where the complications of surveillance lie. The targeted subject may live in a gated community, a secure high-rise, or a close-knit neighborhood, or perhaps you have no address and must find him or her first to even begin the case. All of these factors will attempt to impede your successes and must be conquered to deliver the required results. Surveillance will test your abilities and train you in the same process. Just through offering surveillance services you will build on all facets of your investigative abilities, such as: what are your resources for finding people? Is your car or vehicle stealth enough to go into a neighborhood and stay there all day without being detected? What is your tolerance for waiting long periods of time for activity to occur? If you think little effort will get you results, you're wrong. One of the sciences behind surveillance is to increase your likelihood of seeing your subject. One of the ways to do this is to sit in your position as long as possible. The longer you stay, the greater the chance of seeing your subject. Of course your position, car, and times of surveillance are also all crucial, but if you follow the specific procedures, you will increase your success. If you sit until your subject moves, then how can you not be successful?

So surveillance in its most simplistic form may come down to how much time you are willing to put in—not random periods of time, but consecutive hours. This may be eight, ten, twelve, or longer. Do you have the patience and stamina to wait out your target? Now of course this is, in many cases, the worst-case scenario. The truth is that most people move or are active within an eight-hour day. Another aspect of proper surveillance is to arrive at the target's house early, at least by 6:00 a.m. as a standard start time. No matter what my assignment budget may be, I do not leave until I see my target on the first day of any assignment. This practice takes a lot of pressure off of me, especially if I have the typical two- to three-day time period on a target. This time is assigned to determine the extent of a subject's activity level and general physical capabilities. I never let my objective boil down to the last day. By day three, I usually already know the target's pattern of activity and have video of him or her.

Sticking to the proper procedures for surveillance will prove beneficial for many different objectives. A successful surveillance on a residence can tell you what activity occurs at that location, and the activity can be varied: from being a house of prostitution, a drug house, home-based business, rental property, or just your subject's private homesteaded residence. A good surveillant will also successfully document the comings and goings of all people at that location. If the goal is to document a particular occupant's activity, then the surveillant will be in position to do so unbeknownst to the subject. This also means being able to follow the subject from the residence to anywhere he or she may go.

When attempting to follow someone, your position and egress from the area is crucial. Most targets are lost within the first few minutes of mobile surveillance. The reason for this is that often the surveillant is slightly delayed getting started after the target once he or she leaves. This is a tactical decision, and guessing how much time to give the subject depends on your situation and the layout of the area. Also, a good surveillance vantage point is not always the best position to get out of when the subject moves. Sometimes, when you are sitting in a close-knit area or tight surveillance close to the target, you want him or her to leave and proceed a calculated distance before you start after him or her to maintain discreetness. A miscalculation may cause you to be delayed too long, and your target may proceed away without being followed. When I discuss procedures about following people, it always reminds me of Thomas Magnum in the television series *Magnum PI*. He drove a red Ferrari, and the show depicted him sitting on the street at the end of the target's driveway, and when the target left, he would floor it and peel out in pursuit. Procedurally, cars used in surveillance are nondescript and usually earth tones. We remove any front neighborhood plate or bumper stickers of any sort and avoid having anything on our dashboards that the target may notice and remember during a long tail.

Another TV concept worth thinking about is the suspect looking out the window and seeing a man sitting by himself in a Crown Victoria just outside his or her building.

Proper procedures require an inconspicuous surveillance position outside the direct or peripheral view of your target's house. I always tell my trainees to assume that the target is sitting at his or her bay front window and looking outside. If the subject looks left and right, can he or she spot you? This doesn't mean that you can't be in view, especially if there are other cars present. It just means that the target can't pick your vehicle out of a crowd or pinpoint a concern for your particular vehicle. The spot you choose to set up in might be the single most important start to your case and its eventual success. Never underestimate the importance of choosing a good spot. Can you see the subject's residence? Can you obtain video of him or her from your spot? Can you get out quickly enough from your position to follow the target, regardless of the direction in which he or she leaves? Is your car inconspicuous enough to blend in with the neighborhood?

While most of the cases we work will be on normal law-abiding people, the way we approach each case must be very methodical. I say: approach your case and choice of surveillance location as if your life depends on it. Understand the importance of being discreet, and the results you get will be a reinforcement of how this simple step pays off. After all, our objective is to always enter and exit a neighborhood without anyone knowing that we were there. At the same time though, I'm not saying to park so far away to protect your presence. You must have a visual on the house, driveway, or vehicles to be successful. So it's not as simple as just parking down the street. If the person comes out to pull weeds, cut the lawn, or just get the mail, you need to be in position to document the activity.

Some investigators become lackadaisical when it comes to surveillance. They see it as a mindless activity of sitting—too boring for their degree of talent. These are the same people that get results half the time. Your intensity level and awareness must always stay in high alert. When you let your guard down, that's when you miss some activity or someone spots you.

I recall hiring a young investigator for the rural Tennessee area. Having worked the area myself, I knew that I needed a hunter-type person: someone who could be stealth in the woods and comfortable traversing the terrain of an area where people live on large parcels of land, and getting out of the car is a necessity. This means packing up your gear and going into the woods to get that view of the house and cars on the property.

One of the first cases we worked involved a man living on a large farm. He had lived in Tennessee his whole life, and his property covered the entire side of a small mountain. The plan was to drop Santiago off and have him work his way into the woods to set up an observation post and through two-way radios let me know when our target left and the type of vehicle he was in. My job was to follow the vehicle once it reached the main hard road and follow the target from there to see where he went, what he did, and how he did it. As I drove down the rural country road toward Santiago's drop-off point and began to slow down, Santiago opened the passenger door and rolled out of the vehicle. I was shocked and concerned that he had been hurt. It was our first day together, and I underestimated Santiago's personal experience and intensity for the job. Santiago had been a DOS agent from Colombia, South America. He had come to the United States on political asylum. His job in Colombia was to track the FARC, a rebel, antigovernment group, often involved in drug smuggling and criminal activity of the drug cartel. Santiago's job put his life in danger every day. He learned that his life depended on his actions, and he approached our surveillance work with the same intensity. After I dropped him off, I tried to get in contact with him at the four-hour mark. I tried again at the six-, seven-, and eight-hour time frame. Finally I heard, "Mr. John, come pick me up at the church." This was the original drop-off point, and as I drove the rural road, I saw no Santiago. I drove back down the street, and again I did not see him. Finally I heard, "Mr. John, you keep driving past me." Santiago had been lying flat on the ground in his camouflage clothing, near a large oak tree. Even when exiting the area, he did so with perfect execution. Finally, I said, "Santiago, stand up so I can see you." Santiago secured over two hours of the farmer tending to his animals. The case was a success, and it was because of Santiago's approach and experience. He went on to be the only investigator I know in my thirty years of experience who secured video of a hunter gutting his deer and pulling it down the side of a mountain.

Yesterday, I thought of Santiago as I belly crawled along the side of a playground to get video of a fifty-year-old female executive playing with her grandchild at a playground within a gated upscale West Coast subdivision. Whether in the deep woods of Tennessee or a plush neighborhood, our tactics and intensity have to remain the same. You may think, "how silly," and many would not even try to secure the video or feel it was unimportant or not worth the risk, but this approach has led to many successes, and a philosophy of doing what it takes to get video of all activity whenever possible is my ongoing objective.

Like Santiago, I have learned and perfected my skill of getting out of the vehicle. Many investigators will never exit their cars. Some companies even prohibit their investigators from exiting their vehicles, feeling as a company that their liability risks are less if they keep all investigators in their cars on public roadways. But over the course of my career, I have secured just as much video getting out of my car as I have by remaining in my car. And many times the video I obtained had to be shot out of my car, or there was no way I would have seen the activity. So the combination of the two has made me twice as successful.

Knowing what position to take is usually determined after being on location and having time to evaluate the situation.

I took a case involving a small-town police officer. He was suspected of spending his night shift in the arms or another woman rather than beating the pavement or cruising his designated zone. Looking back on my own policing experience, it wasn't a farfetched suspicion. Since I didn't know which of the several police cruisers he would be using, I started my surveillance from inside the police department's parking area, immediately behind the station. Knowing that he would be arriving for the 11:00 p.m. to 7:00 a.m. shift, I arrived early and positioned myself near the police cruisers. Around the time of the shift change, I had officers all around my vehicle fraternizing with each other as some left and others arrived. The memory still raises the hair on my arms as I recall laying low inside my vehicle with just my eyes high enough over the door panel to keep an eye on my guy as he arrived and went inside to check in, then came out to take control of his assigned car. This was one of the worst cases I worked as I tailed an on-duty police officer, thinking of what might happen to me if he figured out I was following him. I imagined him stopping and searching my car to only mysteriously find some uncontrolled substance that I stopped using decades ago. My stomach rumbled constantly in pain as I followed him around the streets of a small Central Florida community until he decided to hook up with his partner in crime, a single housewife living just blocks from his own home that he shared with his wife.

Being too far away to see what's happening is frustrating, and we always try to work ourselves into a position where we can see every movement. It's challenging, sometimes uncomfortable, and even downright frightening, but it's necessary.

The PI conducts surveillance to develop information or to observe the subject in a "safe" area where the subject believes that he or she is not being watched. Most private investigators will need to have a full understanding of how to conduct proper surveillance. They must be mindful of the laws when conducting investigations, keeping up with federal, state, and local legislation, such as privacy laws and other legal issues affecting their work. The legality of certain methods may be unclear, and investigators must make judgment calls when deciding how to continue a case. They must also know how to collect evidence properly so that they do not compromise its admissibility in court.

In surveillance the power of being invisible is tremendously productive, and it's the constant goal of a PI. Surveillance is a lot more difficult than you might imagine. Bathroom breaks are not an option, and surveillance is ranked as one of the more exhausting investigative activities. Sitting three days on a house, building, or business will drain your brain and body. It is a mental game to see how long you can stay; but at the same time, information is coming to you from all directions. Who comes and goes from the location; how long were they there; what were they carrying; can they be identified; who might they be; and why were they there are all important questions that need to be answered.

You also need to be conscious of your surroundings. At any moment, a neighbor, child at play, or the target may spot you. The mail carrier, meter reader, paper carrier, or casual observer may take notice of your unfamiliar vehicle. But once you make it through all the obstacles, you will mostly likely know everything you need to, or you may know what needs to be done next. You will even obtain information that will be completely useless. Just by sitting and watching, I have seen which house sells drugs or runs prostitution and even which neighbors are cheating with which neighbors. I have watched in amusement as a husband leaves from one household and the wife leaves from another, only to then see the wife from the first house walk over to the husband of the second household. I followed a woman all day once and remained in my vehicle until she finished her class at a local community college, only to see her walk to the parking lot, open her driver's side door, hike up her skirt, squat, and pee. I was no farther than fifteen feet away. Now these observations aren't made by sitting in my driver's seat with my window down and arm hanging out the window. They were made through the careful consideration of knowing where to park and how to remain invisible. I make it a practice to only be in the driver's seat when I am driving. At all other times, I sit in the back, out of view. This is more difficult then it may sound because at a moment's notice you may need to jump into the front seat to drive. And when a person leaves, you have only a few seconds to react. Most people are lost by the PI's delay in getting moving, turned around, or into a position behind the subject to follow him or her. Another practice that I commonly use is to point my vehicle away from the target and their house, business, or location. For instance, if you are in a parking lot facing one direction, I will try to get in a parking space across from yours, facing the opposite direction.

Another surveillance procedure is what I call my three-point approach to performing surveillance. The first is to be in a position in which the subject's door of the location where he or she is staying or visiting is clearly in view. The second is to stay on his or her car when he or she is moving or coming to rest. And the third is to always keep your subject in sight when he or she is in the public, and be prepared to go on foot if he or she is on foot.

In 2008, I received a call from a well-known national restaurant chain based out of Philadelphia. They had allegations of sexual harassment involving one of their VPs. Reportedly, if you were a young, attractive female restaurant manager and didn't welcome his advances, your hopes of moving up the corporate ladder would be affected. They also knew that his expense account often reflected meals away with another party, and it wasn't his fifty-year-old wife traveling with him. He was flying into the Miami airport for the Miami Boat and Yacht Show, and the company wanted me to conduct surveillance on him to see if he was traveling with any other company associate. He also had reservations at the Miami Beach Hilton on North Miami Beach. This was pre-9/11 with access to the airline gates still permissible to welcome arriving passengers. I arrived early, and based on the ID photograph I had of "lover boy," I shot video of him exiting the gate by himself. He didn't leave the gate area though and walked to another gate coming in from Dallas. He stood watching as the passengers exited and moved with a broad smile toward a young twenty-something, curvaceous young woman as she exited the plane. They embraced briefly and then walked through the terminal, deep in conversation. Having identified the two, I made my way to the hotel for their arrival. After an hour, the two checked into the hotel, and for some reason I paused and did not go up in the elevator with them to identify their room. I thought that I could stay in the lobby and pick them back up should they come back down the elevator to leave. Around 9:30 p.m., the two came down for dinner and ate at Don Shula's Restaurant. I followed in behind them and ate. When I saw the menu, though, I realized that my budget on the case did not account for a fifty-dollar steak, so I ordered two servings of crab-stuffed mushroom appetizers, which were only twenty-five dollars. After dinner the two went back upstairs, and I stayed in the lobby bar, watching the 2008 World Series, with my Philadelphia Phillies playing the Tampa Bay Rays. The Phillies, of course, would go on to win the championship.

The next day, I arrived early and sat in the lobby, then realized that I should be up on my subject's floor watching the door because there was also a fourth-floor walkover from the hotel to the beach. I had been talking to one of the security guards, who, for twenty dollars, agreed to get me the room number for "lover boy." With the room number, I proceeded up to the sixth floor and stood in the hallway emergency stairwell as I had done many times, watching down the hall, trying to stay focused on the hotel room door—or where I thought it was. It's challenging work, and several times I exited, just to re-orient myself to the right spot. After staring down a hallway for several hours, you start to lose your sense of depth perception. Making sure you're focused on the right spot on the wall, hall floor, or in this case, a fire extinguisher between their room and the next door, was the only way I knew that I was watching the right door. If they came out and blocked that extinguisher, I would know it was my target.

At around 10:30 a.m., or after what seemed like an eternity, they exited, and I walked out of the stairwell fire escape and made my way to the elevator, joining them. As "lover boy" pushed the tenth floor and looked at me, I nodded like I knew where I was going. Since I had been distracted by the World Series, I had not done my typical survey of the hotel. I had no clue that the hotel had a rooftop pool and restaurant. I followed my subject and his female companion to the roof, where they secured poolside lounge chairs. I went to the atrium restaurant with its dark, tinted windows that overlooked the pool area and sat for the next two hours with my camera sitting plainly on my table up against the glass. My server never knew that it was focused squarely on my targets, documenting their playful love affair in the pool water. Had I not gone back to the key principle of watching the door to the hotel room in this case, I would never have gotten the evidence I needed. I'm not going to tell you that it's easy standing in the stairwell emergency exit with the door opened an inch, peering down a hallway for hours. But the satisfaction you get from doing the job correctly makes the effort well worth it.

Anytime you are watching or following a person, you should have the door, car, or person in view at all times. This simple procedure means that you always start an investigation with a clear starting point of where he or she is. It may be a view of the subject's front door or, in this case, hotel room. Once your subject leaves, either he or she remains in view or the subject's car remains in your view at all times. If the subject parks and goes on foot, you must do the same.

Even the most seasoned professional can make mistakes, and the procedures and guidelines of tailing a person need to be kept fresh in your mind.

I had a case in Newark, NJ, and the investigator I had there worked the case for two days but never saw the subject. Coincidentally, about a week later, I was flying up to Philadelphia for my high school class reunion. So I told my dad that instead of him picking me up in Philly, I would be flying into Newark, which was the same distance for my dad. As long as I flew in and out during daylight hours, dad was fine being my driver. At eighty years young, my father was still always willing to help out. I arrived in the morning, and, like clockwork, there was dad, sitting in the "No Loading" zone outside the baggage claim area. When you're eighty you get away with things that younger people don't. It's a sense that you own the world and have been here longer than those around you. He's slick though and uses it to his advantage. Had an officer even dared to say anything to him, he would have looked around as if he didn't know where he was or that it was a restricted area. He then would have politely started talking about the Eagles, Phillies, or Flyers, just to buy time. Soon enough I would be out, and no harm would be done. I recall driving to the post office, and while I was looking for a spot to park he said, "Just let me out here." By the time I had found a parking spot, he was already coming out of the post office. I said, "It's two weeks before Christmas, with a line halfway out the door. How did you get through that line so quickly? He said, "I just acted like I didn't see the line and walked right up to the counter. If anyone says anything, I'll just look around as if I'm lost." But of course no one feels it's their place to speak out against an eighty-year-old man. I can just imagine the faces of those silent patrons standing in line, thinking, "Poor old guy!"

Well, dad shows up at Newark Airport in a car I've never seen. It seems that every year he has a "new" car. When I say new, I mean new to him. They are usually ten-year-old cars with fewer than fifty thousand miles on them. My dad has preferred to live in a retirement community since he was seventy. For a single guy, it's affordable, and he has a community of friends with like interests. All of us kids have moved to Florida, but for him, the northeast is like nowhere else he would rather be, and the thought of leaving is not a topic of conversation. So he lives in a high-rise retirement building in New Hope, Pennsylvania. With about twenty single women to every man, it's a single man's paradise. He's from an age when women stayed at home and men went to work. In today's world he would be called a male chauvinist, but there is no changing him now. Most of the women there are between seventy-five and ninety years of age, so they put up with his nonsense. Every morning, there is a newspaper slipped under his door by the woman across the hall, who gets the paper just for the crossword puzzle. He has a table stand outside his door to accept dinner plates and leftovers. His refrigerator is so full that there are three-week-old untouched dishes—too many for one man to eat. Desserts, casseroles, meatloaf, and stuffed peppers—it's like living in a hotel with free room service and endless menu choices. But he thinks its normal, and in his defense, when someone needs help, he's always there. He takes the women to their doctors' appointments, and when there's an issue that needs resolving, he goes to the management. He sought and got permission to cultivate a portion of the property for residents to have individual gardens. He contacted the local school to have the students weed the gardens for the seniors as a community service project. He runs the place like it's his private inn, but he is well-respected and appreciated. So it's not uncommon for a ninety-year-old woman who doesn't drive her car any longer to either give or sell it to him. After all, this car will become the new chariot for the manor's chauffer. I called him this past Christmas, only to find that he had been at the hospital for two days. Concerned, I asked, "What happened? Are you all right?" He said that he had to take the woman from down the hall to the hospital, and that she was not doing well.

So at the airport, I admired his new "2007" Lincoln Continental. There's something about older people and their love for big cars. He looked at me proudly and said, "Only forty-seven thousand miles!" I didn't ask who, how, or why; I just said, "From the Manor?" He said, "Yeah."; I said, "Nice."

So our adventure was starting. We left the airport to check out the woman's house where my investigator had seen no activity in two days. The woman lived on a narrow two-way street in a townhouse. We pulled up and parallel parked across the street, just north of the woman's front door. Slanting my dad's rearview mirror, I could see the woman's front door from my position in the front passenger's seat. I noticed that she had Christmas decorations in the windows, with a lit Christmas tree. I thought that this woman was home, and that it was surprising that my Newark investigator never saw her. We arrived there shortly before noon, and around three o'clock, the woman exited the front door and walked in the opposite direction of how we were parked. I yelled at my dad, "There she goes," and he turned to look. I told him to start the car and turn around. Well, he put the car in reverse and backed up two feet, then pulled forward but didn't turn the wheel enough, so we had to back up again. I was watching his right side so that we could clear the car in front, and when he couldn't make the complete turn, we backed up again and started over. The car is big, and with cars parked on both sides, we couldn't make a full U-turn, so he backed up again and turned a little more. We were almost around but didn't have enough clearance with the cars on the other side of the street, so he backed up again. There was a car coming from our left and another coming from our right. The car on the right took advantage of my dad reversing and squeezed around us as we waited in the middle of the road. When my dad finally turned the car around, I had no idea where the woman on foot had gone. We circled the block but didn't see any sign of her. A block in the other direction was the train, and I supposed that she had used the overhead crosswalk to the train. That night we stayed in Newark and avoided talking about the case. I could tell that my dad felt terrible about the situation, but I explained that it was my fault for not jumping out of the car and following her on foot. The next day I remedied the situation and followed her on foot to the train and to the Newark Mall, where she was working in a candle shop for the holiday season—on her feet working when she claimed to be unemployed and incapable of working. After this case, we headed to New Hope, and to celebrate our success I treated my dad to a twenty-ounce Porterhouse steak at the Lambertville Inn.

One of the objectives of a surveillance is to document the activities of the subject without him or her knowing that he or she is being watched. In personal injury cases, video is the documentation that doesn't lie, and people that specialize in just surveillance work are sometimes called surveillance investigators; however, anyone who worked or started out in their career doing a lot of surveillance work will tell you that you grow as an investigator with each surveillance case you work. Many times the subject of your surveillance needs to be located or information and activities observed need to be further documented through collecting evidence and witness statements. It's certain that your talents and investigative knowledge and ability will grow with each case.

Since video evidence is so important, we should talk about the use of your camcorder. When you're taking video, you must train your camera to stay on the subject of your investigation. Taking fifteen minutes of video during your investigation, ten minutes of which is nothing but your subject's home or car will never be enough. In surveillance, it's important to remember that your goal is to document your subject's movement and behavior by using video. That means getting video of the activities your subject is engaged in. Video of houses, cars, or people not directly relevant to your investigation will not be of any help to you or your client. It's up to you as a professional private investigator to take this untrained video camera and teach it to perform to your specifications by recording the subject under surveillance. You should know that surveillance video of less than five or ten minutes will, for the most part, be considered inadequate for most investigative evidence purposes.

Video cameras have come a long way, and I can recall the early days when the video recorder was a reel-to-reel machine with an attached camera on a cord. Even after several years of progress, most video systems were still two-piece units, where the camera was separate from the recording device. This situation created a cumbersome problem in the fact that it limited where you could go with the device. With the introduction of the one-piece camera and recorder combination called the "camcorder," the ability to conceal your video camera was increased tremendously. The camcorder was readily concealable and extremely portable so it could be used in a variety of hidden applications. Today, microchip technology has created body-worn pinhole cameras that enable covert videoing on secure digital high capacity (SDHC) memory cards or miniature DVRs with hard drives half the size of a pack of cigarettes. The options that you have in concealing such units are almost limitless, considering their size. Companies like Super Circuits out of Austin, Texas, have long been a source for affordable covert equipment. They sell surveillance cameras hidden in clocks, radios, fire alarms, emergency light systems, stereos, books, briefcases, garbage cans, fence posts, power transformers, picture frames, loose-leaf binders, lamps, radar detectors, and even mailboxes. Some nanny applications even call for hiding video cameras in stuffed animals. Because of advanced chip technology and the miniaturization of the video camera, the possibilities for securing video anywhere is almost limitless.

As a surveillance investigator, your camera is your weapon. You must be comfortable and knowledgeable in its use and applications. Practice shooting video by going to a busy shopping center or grocery store and video people coming and going from their car to the store entrance and as they exit and walk to their car. Many camcorders may be equipped with a red, flashing LED light mounted on the front or top of the camcorder. This light called the "tally light" indicates that the camera is in the recording mode. It can usually be turned off in the camera's "settings" mode. If it cannot be turned off, you will want to put a small piece of black electrical tape over the LED light on the camcorder before conducting any surveillance investigation. This, once again, will allow you to video your subject without anyone around you being aware of the fact that your camera is on. The camera will also record sound while recording, which you will want to eliminate. To do this, simply plug a jack "stud" in the microphone port of the camera. The stud will be a nonworking microphone jack connector with no wires attached and will disconnect the built-in microphone on the camera. Before utilizing your camcorder or any video surveillance equipment, read, in detail, the instructions accompanying the equipment. Once again, it is important that you familiarize yourself with any equipment before ever attempting to utilize it in the field. Whenever I get a new camera, I keep the manual with me while I'm on surveillance and read through the manual page by page to ensure that I have a complete and thorough understanding of my camera's features and operation.

You will use surveillance often for many different types of investigations. Your comfort level with your equipment is fundamental to your success. You sometimes only have one chance to secure valuable evidence, so be ready. It's hard to deny a fact or activity caught on video, and learning how to creatively capture video evidence will be an ongoing challenge.

PRACTICE MAKES PERFECT

Using different pieces of video equipment from high-powered lenses to miniature covert cameras will be a routine part of many field investigations. In this day and age, proving a case can be challenging, and people want proof. They want to see the activity and hold the evidence. As investigators, if we say that the subject was creating fraudulent appraisals or producing phony tax returns, we not only need the papers, but we had better have video of the subject actually filling out the papers. Having good equipment is just part of the process; being proficient in its use is the challenge.

I carry several miniature covert cameras: one uses a regular, full-size secure digital (SD) memory card, while the other smaller devices use micro SD cards. I'll use different cameras for different applications because some react to light differently. Some capture low-light activity, while others fail entirely in a similar situation. Some have sensitive auto irises that don't react well with fluctuation in light levels like you find in a disco or nightclub setting, where there may be a strobe light. Knowing which camera to use in different circumstances comes with testing and sometimes on-the-job trial and error.

When possible, I prefer to use my button-hole camera, which is hardwired to a miniature digital video recorder (DVR) with a color screen. I will place the DVR in my front pocket and periodically take it out to view the screen and see what I am recording.

For non-covert field use, I have a newer hard disk camera with multiple SD memory card ports that enable me to shoot upwards of forty hours of video without a single download. My preference for a surveillance camera has been and will be a Canon product. I recommend always having at least two hard-drive cameras in your surveillance bag. I do not believe that anyone should still be using a camera that takes a tape. A tape camera has too many moving parts, and the quality is inferior to the newer cameras. I always tell my trainees to buy the digital cameras secondhand online through websites like eBay. People often buy or are given video cameras for presents, only to find they don't use them often enough to want to keep them. So the secondhand market has very reasonably priced midgrade cameras for starting out. I don't recommend paying more than $150.00 for a suitable starter camera. Some of the older Canon non-HD models with no built-in hard drive and using only an SD memory card for recording make perfect surveillance cameras, and you can buy one for around $100.00–$125.00. Whatever model you choose, make certain you can afford to have two cameras.

The quality of the lens your camera has is an extremely important part of your choice of which camera to buy. For surveillance situations, look for a camera with the highest optical zoom capacity. Using the right camera enables the investigator to distance himself or herself from the subject of the surveillance. The use of a camera with an enhanced optical lens should enable you to shoot video of a subject from around fifty to seventy-five yards away. This video should clearly ID the subject in the video footage from this distance.

Many camera models emphasize the digital zoom power; however, this should not be a deciding factor in your purchase. We do not use digital zoom technology during surveillance. This technology merely takes the pixels of an image and enhances them electronically by splitting and filling in the spaces to make the image look larger, but the quality is greatly depleted. This poor quality image, coupled with the need to stream it over the Internet to your client, will make your efforts look more like a mosaic piece of art rather than a surveillance video. So remember, we *never* use the digital zoom technology, and we shut this feature off in the main camera settings.

Never use the automatic focus functions on your camcorder when videoing. The automatic focus should be used before you film just to set the correct focus for the distance you are shooting. Once the focusing distance is set, turn *off* the auto focus. This is important because your camcorder automatically focuses on the nearest object to the camcorder's lens. This means that if a person, motor vehicle, a leaf, a bush, a fly, or even a speck of dust comes between your lens and the subject you're videoing, the camcorder will refocus on this interference until it passes. It will then self-adjust to try to regain focus of your subject. This simple mistake can cause you to miss valuable and irreplaceable video.

Finally, your camera should come equipped with "image stabilization" technology. This cuts down on any minor movement caused by free-holding the camera.

Camera Specifications
1. Lens capacity (highest optical resolution)
2. Image stabilizer
3. Manual focus button

Remember that the camcorder is an important piece of the professional investigator's equipment. While cameras have come down in costs, they are still an investment that needs to be cared for properly. Your camcorder can be affected by moisture, extreme heat, extreme cold, and sudden temperature changes. Therefore, you should never leave your camcorder in your vehicle in the sun and heat for the entire day. Treat it like your pet: it'll die if improperly cared for or subjected to abuse and neglect. Never leave your camcorder in your vehicle overnight. Your vehicle is never a safe or secure place to leave expensive equipment or valuable evidence.

The stock camera battery that comes with most cameras usually lasts just one hour. Your camera battery can always be upgraded to a two-hour battery. Remember to remove the battery from your device during periods of inactivity when the camera is not in use. If you charge your battery to its full capacity the evening before conducting the surveillance and attach it to your camera in the case, when you set out to use the device the next morning, you could lose some of the battery's capacity. Remember to leave your battery unattached until you're ready to use it. Always have a second and maybe even a third fully charged battery as part of your accessories. You never know when you may need to shoot a full day's activity, so be prepared. Always take your charger with you so that you can be recharging a battery while using another. Also, have several extra memory cards in case some unforeseen problem arises—like a memory card giving you a formatting error.

You will need to invest in a camcorder cigarette-lighter battery cord. In this manner, the camcorder can be operated via a cigarette-lighter battery cord, using your automobile battery as your source for power. Your camcorder batteries can then be utilized when you leave your vehicle, giving you the maximum benefit of portability. Using your power sources in this manner will increase your effectiveness. Most cameras also serve as chargers now, so with the cigarette battery cord, you can charge a battery in one camera while using the other. This is also a good time to mention that the second camera you carry on surveillance should be of the same make and model so that it uses the same batteries.

Power converters are also a necessity and will enhance overall charging, restoring a battery back to its full power quicker than the conventional cigarette-lighter charger. It also serves as a means of power for your tablet, laptop, or other devices.

The tripod is another important piece of equipment. One of the most common client complaints about surveillance video is that it is too shaky or out of focus. These are factors that can be avoided with a better understanding of your camera's function and by using a tripod or monopod. There are several factors that can cause shaky video: First, you may be recording your subject for an extended period of time, often as long as an hour or more. It's difficult to hold a camcorder still for ten minutes, let alone an hour. A tripod or monopod, extending from the base of your camera, will allow you to steady the camera. Second, if you're conducting surveillance from your vehicle, make sure that you turn your engine off while recording. It won't always be comfortable without air-conditioning, but the vibration caused by your running engine will adversely affect your video recording. If for some reason you don't have a tripod, it's important to use good video technique. Shooting steady video can also be accomplished by using a rest or supporting the camera with both hands. Both elbows should be parallel to each other and tucked toward the middle of your chest. By holding the camcorder in this manner, you're allowing your skeletal structure to support the weight of the camcorder, instead of your muscles and tendons. If you hold the camcorder with one hand, flaring your elbow out to the side, your arms will inevitably become tired and start to shake, especially when you're recording for long periods of time. Using the proper recording technique that we've discussed will allow you to get clear and steady video evidence in almost any situation. However, you should always have and use a tripod for any extended video recording.

Let's recap the operation of your camcorder:
1. Always charge your batteries before leaving the house and don't leave a battery in a camera that is not in use.
2. Know your camera before you attempt to use it in the field.
3. Always turn your camera to "manual focus" before filming.
4. Paranoia has no place in filming. Remember that your camera is pre-trained to record dashboards, floorboards, and trees. You must train your camera to stay on the subject under surveillance, no matter what happens. Keep your subject's head at the top of the screen and his or her feet at the bottom.
5. Don't try to review your film in the field until your entire investigation is complete in order to ensure no accidental erasure takes place.

6. Don't use an outdated camera that needs a tape.
7. Purchase affordable secondhand cameras that use SD memory card technology or have built-in digital hard drives.
8. Always have two regular video cameras in your bag and one or two covert cameras.

Practice using your equipment because it takes familiarity to use the equipment in a more stressful environment. To get better at obtaining video evidence and the feel for surveillance work, I recommend that you go to a supermarket and video a person going inside and then as they come out. Try following them to see how long you can stay with them. Surveillance and videoing together is an art that you will only learn to get better at over time. You can also practice by going into a neighborhood and picking up a target vehicle to follow out of the area to see where it goes. If they stop at a convenience store, are you able to start your filming just before they exit their vehicle? If not, what can you do to increase your readiness? Getting video of a person exiting his or her vehicle and going into a store is a piece of documentation a seasoned investigator will obtain and something that the agency will look for to access your talent.

An experienced manager can usually tell how long you have been in the field just by reviewing your video. When I see less-than-acceptable video, I think one of two things: this investigator is new to the industry or, the worst-case scenario, this investigator doesn't care about the quality of his or her work product. As you start out, focus on quality, *not* quantity; five minutes of great video is better than ten minutes of blurry or shaky video. Another suggestion is to take your camera into a wooded forest area and see if you can stay for several hours. Focus your camera on a subject matter and keep it recording for two hours. The time you spend in the woods will be a good exercise to teach you what may be needed to spend an extended period of time out of your car.

INSURANCE FRAUD

As we continue to better understand how to fight fraud, states, too, progressively develop better laws. However, not all states consider insurance claim fraud a felony. I remember not too long ago when it was difficult to get an insurance fraud case prosecuted. At first insurance fraud cases involving material misrepresentation and deception were reviewed by the state or county prosecutor's office. Often these prosecutors and their criminal investigators found it difficult to justify using their resources for what they felt to be a civil matter or less serious crime. After all, our state and county prosecutors didn't just handle fraud cases; they handled burglaries, robberies, auto thefts, murders, assaults, and other violent crimes. We used to have to go to great lengths to get a prosecutor to look at an insurance fraud case when they had "bigger fish to fry." Pursuing an accident victim lying or exaggerating about the extent of his or her injuries was not what most prosecutors saw as a high-priority case. However, this changed when insurance companies lobbied Congress for stricter laws against people who fabricated, exaggerated, or outright devised criminal schemes to defraud insurance companies. Many states formed special departments to handle insurance related crimes.

In Florida, the Divisions of Insurance Fraud (DIF) was established and staffed with special prosecutors and investigators focused solely on fighting insurance fraud. In return, many states required the insurers to better evaluate, identify, and investigate these acts so that they could be referred to the state's investigative bodies for criminal prosecution. It was a fair trade-off with insurance companies responsible for conducting the initial investigative work until substantial evidence was found to warrant a referral to the state. The insurance industry started to beef up its investigative forces, which today are referred to as the Special Investigative Unit (SIU). In Florida, any insurance company having reached one million dollars in insurance premiums must have a defined investigative plan and SIU department to identify and investigate fraud. Many PIs specialize in assisting the SIU in conducting insurance-related investigations. Working for the insurance industry means a steady flow of business and, if done well, job security. SIUs are usually made up of a dozen investigators per company per state. They handle and manage investigations conducted by their own staff and the much larger number of investigators they contract with through private investigative firms. The insurance companies' staff investigators are exempt from the licensing requirement, which means that there are thousands of SIU investigators that are not calculated in the PI statistics. According to the International Association of SIU (IASIU) membership, as of 2013, they reported four thousand members, representing six hundred different insurance companies.

When fraud is suspected and investigated, the completed report and evidence is submitted to the Florida Department of Agriculture and Consumer Services, Division of Financial Services. A state law enforcement officer is then assigned to the case and will review the referral, meet with the investigator, and verify the facts and evidence submitted for review and, hopefully, for criminal prosecution under the insurance fraud statutes. Once a case has been submitted, we will receive a formal letter for the collection of all reports, evidence, and video we have so that the file can be reviewed for possible criminal prosecution. The letters will typically state: "In compliance with the requirements of Section 934.43, Florida Statutes, your company has referred information to the Division that an insurance related crime has or may have occurred that could result in the filing of criminal charges."

Section 626.989(6), Florida Statutes, also requires that your company, in addition to sending the initial report or information regarding suspected criminal activity, send "such additional information relative thereto as the department may require."

Please take note that this request relates to an official criminal investigation of a suspected felony. Given that, you are not to disclose the existence of this request to the subject of this investigation. Such disclosure could obstruct and impede the investigation being conducted and thereby interfere with the enforcement of the law, in violation of Section 934.43, Florida Statutes.

Over the years private investigative firms and state law enforcement officers have improved their coordination and communications. In 1992, at the Hilton Hotel in Altamonte Springs, the Florida Insurance Fraud Education Committee (FIFEC) began its existence as the first joint Department of Insurance Fraud DIF/SIU Annual Conference.

In 1999, my office had just finished a case that we had referred to the DIF. This same case was used as a teaching tool at the educational conference and caught the attention of the ABC network's consumer investigative division. They wanted to do a story on workers' compensation scams, and our case was a perfect example. The inserted picture is a still image taken from the actual video footage. We had over ten hours of video from an investigation that took several months. The subject first needed to be located and then identified as he had changed his name to avoid detection. The story ABC broadcasted was called "Money for Nothing," by Greg Hunter. Below is a short excerpt from the story:

Millions of Americans claim on-the-job injuries every year, but not all are telling the truth. The director of business development at Claims Resource Inc., a nationwide investigation firm, says some workers don't give it too much thought. "They can be your average person, just thinking that it's an easy way for them to make some money. Do they realize what kind of a crime they're committing? I don't think they think about it," he said.

"From Bad Shoulder to a Wrestling Ring"
Leroy Howard of St. Petersburg, FL, hurt his right shoulder moving heavy furniture and could not work, receiving workers' compensation benefits. But the Claims Resource investigator found the six-foot-two, 250-pound man working in the ring as a professional wrestler, known as "The Navy Seal." The Seal was no match for the investigator's camera, which revealed that Howard's "injury" did not appear to be hindering his performance.
Meanwhile, Howard, the wrestler, said that getting caught actually helped him focus on a new direction. He is in college and looks forward to life outside the ring.

Fraud is a major crime that imposes significant financial and personal costs on individuals, businesses, government, and society. On one level, insurance fraud is an economic crime, but fraud also is a violent crime that can involve murder, personal injury, and serious property damage. Nearly $80 billion in fraudulent claims are made annually in the United States, according to the Coalition Against Insurance Fraud (CAIF). This figure includes all lines of insurance, and it's also a conservative figure because many insurance fraud cases go undetected and unreported. Fraud schemes and swindlers prey on victims of virtually every race, income, age, education level, and region of the United States.

According to the CAIF, forty-nine states currently have insurance claim fraud as a criminal violation, with forty-three of those states classifying it as a felony. Only fifteen states nationwide currently require insurance companies to have an SIU department. The trend clearly indicates that fighting fraud saves hundreds of millions of dollars annually, so as more states require insurers to adopt the SIU program, more private investigative jobs will result. The US Department of Labor and Statistics further supports this trend as they project investigations as a career path to be one of the fastest growing professions across all occupations.

LABOR OF LOVE

n 1954 George Wackenhut, a former FBI special agent started a Miami-based private investigative agency called "Special Agents Investigations, Inc." In 1958 it was renamed The Wackenhut Corporation, and by the early 1980s, The Wackenhut Corporation employed more than twenty thousand employees but had transitioned from its original private investigator beginnings to offering guard and security services.

As the tools of the security industry changed, separate divisions within their own organizations gave rise to creating special units for conducting investigations. Investigations were not as cut-and-dried as the early years of security work detail. A security officer's responsibilities were often specific in nature with tasks of protecting property or valuables. Often, assignments were to transfer valuables or take a person from point *A* to point *B*. It was understood how much time it would take, and the talent to conduct the task was plentiful. But in investigations, the tasks or results sought were not as easily calculated for costs. It may take longer than anticipated—much longer. The trail of leads may be widespread and require extensive traveling. The equipment needed might not be defined until the case is started. There were so many variables that it was often difficult to quote a client the costs of an assignment. On top of material costs, you also had the gumshoe: the guy on the street, in a car, tracking down leads. George Wackenhut was not the first to find the difficulties in setting up an investigative company nor would he be the last. Investigative efforts still largely depended on "a body" in the field or one analyzing the data. The job cannot be as easily automated as perhaps securing cargo with a safe, armored car or providing security at a bank or business with video cameras and a security alarm.

In 2002, Wackenhut, which refocused its primary business away from investigations to security and guard service, was subsequently purchased by G43, the world's largest security company, measured by revenues with operations in around 125 countries. With over 620,000 employees, it is reportedly the world's third-largest private sector employer.

Another formidable name, with contributions to the private investigations industry was Retail Credit, which, in 1901, saw providing investigative reports and information to the health care industry as a fast-growing business. The company would later change its name to Equifax and would also become part of the investigative era as they conducted in-field surveys, later referred to as Activity Checks, Wellness Checks, Personal Contacts and Dependency Checks. The nature of the inquiries was to determine various aspects of a policyholder's activities as they related to the benefits that they would receive or were receiving as a result of a personal insurance policy, work policy, or spousal coverage.

For instance, let's say that a person had an insurance policy for disability, yet during the inquiry, the investigator found that the subject was not at home, and a conversation with the neighbor determined that the subject worked as an automobile mechanic in his own shop down the street. Depending on the coverage or stipulation of the policy, it may only pay benefits while the subject is unable to work or while he is unable to find work. There are many different types of policies for different types of coverage, which, in turn can all be investigated. Equifax had a great idea and was onto something, but like Wackenhut, they saw more money in another area of business. Equifax would concentrate on collecting personal information and data-mining, creating one of the largest information services business in the United States. They would introduce the "Credit Report," and much later, they also contributed an investigative report called the comprehensive background report, sold under the company name Choice Point. Choice Point combined personal data sourced from public and private databases for sale to the government and private sector. The firm maintained more than seventeen billion records of individuals and businesses, which it sold to an estimated one hundred thousand clients, including seven thousand federal, state, and local law enforcement agencies (30 March 2005 estimates). Private investigative agencies also had accounts through Choice Point, enabling them to access this same information.

Both of these behemoth companies found their way out of the traditional private investigative business. They both found challenges in preserving a profitable or scalable business based solely on conducting private investigations. Conquering the concern over a limited market and operating in a high cost, labor-intensive industry was the challenge. Through their efforts it was proven that the health care industry could provide a sustainable market. With the efficiencies data collection and comprehensive reports provided, investigators could save valuable field time, making them more productive and efficient. The 1980s would bring about a new era of boutique investigative agencies, offering mostly statewide coverage but specifically structured to service the insurance industry. This *new* industry and career path would open the door to a new era of the modern private investigator.

COMPENSATION

The salary and benefits of a staff private investigator's position will vary from state to state and from agency to agency. You'll find all the typical benefits expected from any well-run corporation. Typically, you will receive one week's vacation after the first year, followed by two weeks the second and three weeks after five years. Most companies won't want you to take all three weeks at one time; however, this may vary from agency to agency. Of course, there will be sick pay—usually four days a year—and a 401 K or similar retirement plan. A good ballpark estimate of what you will make starting out hourly will be around eighteen dollars an hour. You can expect to progress through your career with promotions and raises for an increased hourly raise of between twenty-five dollars to thirty-five dollars an hour. Of course all your expenses are on top of that hourly wage. They will offer a car allowance or mileage reimbursement of around fifty cents per mile. We put on a lot of miles, and while the mileage reimbursement is fair, you will need to watch your expenses carefully and take care of your vehicle to get as many miles as you can. According to AAA, the average costs to operate a motor vehicle rose in 2012 by 1.1 cents per mile to 59.6 cents per mile, or $8,946 per year, based on fifteen thousand miles of annual driving. PIs can drive twice that many miles per year, so the average costs will be much higher. I have always made sure to get regular oil changes and find that I can get over 120,000 miles on any car I purchase, which in recent years lasts me around five years.

Some companies find that they can pay their investigators less in an hourly rate by providing an investigator a car and gas card. This takes some of the financial burden off the newly hired investigator. Having run a business myself, I find this not a particularly attractive path as the expenses associated with this approach run high for the company. They now own a fleet of vehicles and must insure the drivers and vehicles. Maintenance costs will still apply; gas charges and mileage must be monitored; and in general, an employee won't take as good of care of a car he or she doesn't own.

Any time the company cuts a responsibility from an employee, they must absorb it in administrative or supervision time. Less responsibility usually means less money for the PI. As a manager, I preferred to keep as much responsibility in the hands of my investigators. Working as a staff investigator might not make you rich, but it can be a rewarding career. I also said "might not" make you wealthy because I will add that I know many staff investigators who have done well for themselves because of their fieldwork experience and ability to recognize an opportunity and capitalize on it. I also believe that the thoroughness and work ethic necessary to become a good investigator are also the driving forces behind an investigator's ability to build personal wealth.

Many smaller companies in the investigative industry use subcontracted investigators who use their own vehicle and equipment. The agency pays the investigator an hourly rate and mileage or some daily stipend for the use of his or her vehicle. These investigators usually have at least two years of experience and are familiar with the workings of the industry. If this option is presented to you as a newly starting investigator, you may want to take advantage of the opportunity to gain experience while perhaps looking for a better and more stable position with a larger company. At the same time, if you have that entrepreneurial spirit, you never know if perhaps this may be a company that you have entered on the ground floor and have the opportunity to assist in the growth of the company and reap the rewards of its future success. When I joined my first company, there were just four investigators.

Larger companies prefer to control more of the moving parts of its operation. They don't mind the added administrative time if they get the desired results. First, they hire only full-time staff, typically recruiting recent college graduates. They put them on a salary of between six hundred to seven hundred dollars a week and cover all expenses. The company buys and assigns all equipment to the investigator to prevent the concern of an investigator in the field with faulty or broken equipment. So to ensure well-equipped investigators, companies take control of the purchase and maintenance of all equipment.

As a young professional, visit the company's corporate office if the opportunity presents itself. Look for a company that has had investigators on staff more than fifteen years. When you are called for an interview, you should be impressed by the manager's poise and knowledge. The person interviewing you would typically be an investigative manager who spent many years in the field and now supervises others. He or she will be or should be very confident and able to answer all of your questions. To put it frankly, he or she should impress you as a leader and a sharp businessperson.

JOB DETAIL

With insurance and insurance defense industry being one of the largest contractors of investigative services, you'll find most investigative agencies advertise insurance investigations. Many times it may not be their specialty or area of expertise, but the amount of work that the insurance industry generates eventually reaches every agency in one way or another.

All hopeful investigators are students of ongoing learning, problem solvers, resourceful, and persistent. We learn the basic concepts of interviewing, background-check procedures, locate techniques, and surveillance. An investigator hired out of college will be trained by his or her employer to perform services according to that company's expertise and procedures. There are so many different types of jobs that the PI may specialize in, that it's incumbent upon the employer to train the PI in the manner in which they want things done. Even trained investigators with a law enforcement background need to be retrained for work in the private sector. Those that come from specialized fields and bring those talents to the private industry also need to learn how to transition their expertise to the private sector and market. An example of this may be a computer programmer or systems engineer that decides to offer his or her computer forensics talents to the public. He or she may offer services to uncover deleted e-mails on a computer to prove infidelity.

In many complex investigations, specialists are brought in or consulted as part of the entire investigation. A suspected electrical fire may warrant an electrical engineer being hired. A stolen vehicle with a broken steering column or faulty brakes may need to be inspected by a mechanic or mechanical engineer. Some investigators may have backgrounds in these areas, but you can't be a specialist in all areas. We must learn to identify and collect evidence in many different types of cases. Just because you're not a specialist doesn't mean you won't be counted on to assist or even gather, store, save, or ship evidence. This evidence is then sent to those experts who can offer their expertise. Many times, we just need to call the professionals and ask them, "How do you want this specimen sent to you for evaluation so that it is not contaminated?"

Recently, I had a case involving a subject who used the drive-through at a fast-food restaurant. An hour later he reported that he sucked a piece of debris up the straw of his closed soda drink. He opened the lid to find an undetermined foreign mass about the size of a dime. He became sick to his stomach and immediately went to the hospital. Statements were taken from the subject, and a full examination was done of the restaurant where he used the drive-through. How could a foreign substance have gotten into his drink? The ice machine in the back of the restaurant showed signs of wear, and the door did not close tightly, leaving gaps for infiltration and contamination. A large white bucket was sitting on top of the ice machine and was used to carry the ice from the back room ice maker to the front drive-through ice-and-drink dispenser. The cups used were stored behind the restaurant in a shed that was not air-conditioned. There were many areas where contamination could have infiltrated the process. The specimen was collected and sent to the University of Florida for diagnosis. Prior to sending the specimen, we were instructed specifically by the lab on how to package and send the specimen. We aren't expected to know everything, but we are expected to ask and follow directions. Many of our cases are unique and call for different types of procedures. But don't get lost in the technicality of things; just move forward and do your best to get the task handled. The concern we had for the foreign substance in the patron's drink was whether it was poisonous to humans. Could this substance be identified and determined if it would cause any future problems? The UF lab determined the foreign mutilated object to be a green tree frog, nontoxic and harmless to humans.

Almost anyone could have carried out this investigation. When working any case, it is not uncommon to offer a follow-up suggestion. In this case, after the field investigation and collection of the specimen, the follow-up was offering to find a private lab and have the foreign substance tested and identified. Because of this case, I now have a private lab to add to my list of contacts for future cases.

Many different types of cases will involve talking to people to gather the facts of what happened. You should always get as many details as possible so that you can continue to confirm the story. The more information you get, the more opportunities you have to verify the story, and eventually you will have the ability to draw a conclusion. As investigators, we want to understand the story then set out to confirm it by gathering corroborating pieces of information or evidence so our conclusion has a high degree of certainty. The more information and pieces we get to the puzzle, the picture of what happened appears clearer, even if some pieces are still missing.

As a PI in the insurance claims industry, I find myself working slip-and-falls, employee fights, workplace accidents, and any incident where a business may face issues of liability, such as the frog case. I also work cases were fraud and questionable business practices costs businesses and insurance companies money such as disreputable auto repair establishments, fraudulent automobile glass replacement scams, and medical clinics fraud schemes, just to name a few. That's the commercial side of claims. Then I also work "personal lines," which means incidents involving the insurance carriers' customers making claims on personal policies for storm damage, auto accidents, stolen vehicles, accidents on their personal property, dog bites, arsons, burglary, and home break-ins. And the list goes on with many other possible assignments. One day you may be investigating something to do with truck drivers; the next day, a doctor. And being a PI also means that you will get those calls from people outside your typical circle to work other matters.

My friend Phil, who owns a PI Agency in New Jersey, called me with a case referral. He said, "John, I can't tell you the client's name. He's a powerful person here in NJ." We are part of these conversations all the time, and we usually still tell each other who the person is. Our clients always think they're special, but we get many well-known and wealthy people as clients all the time. After all, they are the ones who can afford our services. They are also usually well-educated and realize the importance of hiring an investigator for the information we can provide. But Phil was acting differently with this one, and he wasn't budging on a name. He almost had me concerned, but somewhere between my five-thousandth case and my ten-thousandth case, the politics of a client were no longer a concern to me. So Phil went on with the facts of the case, reporting that this client had met a Miami escort through the telephone book in his hotel room while staying at the Mandarin Oriental Hotel in Miami. He had been seeing her for some time, and she had agreed to stop working in return for the $15,000 a month he sent her. These types of relationships were not uncommon in Miami—or perhaps all over the world—where there is a pool of beautiful woman.

This case took me back to when I was perhaps one year into my career as a PI. I was sitting surveillance in Miami Beach and noted a beautiful young woman walking across the parking lot. I couldn't help but watch her, but then she, too, had those wandering eyes. We made eye contact, followed by a lonely smile. A cab was waiting to take her to the store, and when she returned, she saw that I was still there. I had no choice; I was working, but when she invited me up to her apartment, a twenty-two-year-old guy's dedication can only take so much temptation. I figured I could work my case any day, so it didn't have to be that day. I locked the door of my hot, stuffy car and sought out the ocean breeze of a ninth-floor condominium. She soon told her story of being a kept woman that was only visited perhaps once a month by her supporting unnamed out-of-town sugar daddy.

So the NJ referral was not a foreign topic to me. I had some knowledge in this area, and getting this case fifteen years later as a more mature investigator made playing a role easier.

The New Jersey client suspected that his young kept Cuban concubine was not holding up her end of the business arrangement. He suspected that she was still operating as an escort and wanted proof. I was given her mobile number, which she had seemingly kept for the past five years. I was instructed to check into the Mandarin Oriental Hotel Concierge level—four hundred dollars a night—and call her from my hotel room. The key to getting information or getting someone to do what you want is to be convincing. When we pretend to be someone we are not, it is called using a "pretext." Being able to act out a role is an important skill for the PI. The delivery of your pretext must be believable, and you don't get second chances. It is important that you have the details of your ruse concrete and worked out in your head to answer every probable question.

Being believable is such an important part of being a successful investigator that I have passed it down to my youngest son. He has heard about so many cases that I believe he is qualified to be a PI through osmosis. In 2009, my youngest son and I were running a nonprofit basketball organization formed to offer young males the opportunity to play AAU basketball. Between tournaments I took the entire team back to my house to rest. Later that evening, a player's gold chain came up missing, and even though all the players were teammates, there was clearly a thief among us. Initially, I hoped it had been put in the wrong duffel bag by accident, but it hadn't. I asked my son to investigate the incident and focus in on what he knew about every player on the team. One player, in particular, who was new to the team, and didn't seem very sympathetic about the situation, became the leading suspect. I was off to Miami, so my son came up with a plan to tell the team that we had hidden cameras in the house, and that the cameras had caught the thief on *video*. He asked for the chain to be returned anonymously, and no action would be taken. He then took it one step further, and without the other players knowing, he confronted the one player he suspected. My son stated that he was nervous, but I told him that it would only work if he looked confident and, in this case, disappointed with what the teammate had done. I told him to picture what the teen had done before confronting him. Once confronted, the teen admitted to taking the chain, and it was returned anonymously as my son had each team member go back to the room one by one and again search their duffel bags.

So now back to the escort story that I know you are wondering about. When I got to the Mandarin Oriental and prepared to call Monique, I knew what I was going to say. I had prepared it in my mind, but I was also prepared to ad-lib when necessary. This was not my first assignment, and I was far from being nervous. I called, and she answered the phone. I stated that I had been coming to Miami for many years and had seen her ad sometime back and had stored her number in my phone. I joked and said that I was surprised it was still good. We talked about my occupation, and I used my real name, as I usually do in most cases. She told me that she was busy this weekend and to call her next week. I was told that if she was busy, I was to set up surveillance on her house and see what she did. That night she was picked up by a black Town Car and taken to the Hollywood Beach Hilton. There was a nightclub on the ground floor, but she headed directly to the elevator and got in. I sat in the lobby till 1:00 a.m., but she never came down. I ended up going back to her house off Hallandale Beach Boulevard. She lived in an older cottage home with a garage and alleyway behind the house. Sitting in the back alleyway was a large gray trash container that was sitting out for collection. Inside her trash receptacle, I found three full white plastic trash bags. I pulled all three and quickly tossed them into the back of my vehicle.

I went through the trash a few miles from the address. Inside were credit card charge receipts for several male clients. There were also photocopies of matching drivers' licenses. The amounts were the telltale sign that she was still in business. My client had told me her rate was five hundred dollars an hour, with a two-hour minimum, but it was obvious that she worked for less, as most of the charges were for just five hundred dollars.

By 1:30 a.m. Monique was still not home, and I ended my surveillance efforts. I had enough information to report back to my client. But he wanted more positive proof. He wanted video and started dishing out more money. Over the next three weeks I kept in contact with her and conducted more surveillance. One weekend she left for the Bahamas; another evening she met a male for dinner then met a girlfriend and went out partying on Las Olas Boulevard in Fort Lauderdale. Finally, her schedule was free, and she agreed to meet me at the Mandarin Oriental Hotel. The client wanted video of her coming and going from the hotel, so I needed to employ a second investigator for the evening. Guys that are accustomed to using "call girls" report that there is a thrill in the activity. It's not the service or the sex; it's that "knock on the door" when you don't know what to expect. I was completely fine throughout this whole process and never hesitated to make the call, follow her, or do what I needed to do for the case. But when she knocked on the door, my heart started to beat rapidly. From this point forward, I couldn't plan. She was a beautiful young Latin woman around twenty-five years old, five feet ten inches tall, with a curvaceous body and large bust. We introduced ourselves, and fortunately I used my real name because the first thing she asked for was my driver's license. After a brief introduction, she went directly to the minibar and opened two bottles of scotch and poured them into her glass. As we sat and talked, she started to tell me about her arrangement with the out-of-town businessman. She said that she needed to stay with him for five years, and then she would have enough money to retire. She had been investing the money and felt certain that she was in control of the situation. It brought back memories of the woman from Miami that I had met a decade and a half earlier. But in this instance, the circumstances were very different, and the young woman had no idea that I was working for her sugar daddy. As agreed, I handed her the five hundred dollars, and I thanked her for her time. As she left my room, I called the investigator in the lobby to prepare to secure video of her leaving. This was our proof that she had come and gone and had spent time in my room.

Once an investigation is completed, we rarely hear about the outcome. I can only surmise that my client finally realized that he was being taken. But in actuality, I needed to be focused on my next case and not dwell on the last one because I have yet to find a sugar mamma willing to keep me.

You will hear many times that as a private investigator, you are a constant student, learning about different lines of businesses and activities and, through surveillance, constantly studying people and their "patterns of behavior." The more you watch people, the more you learn about the likelihood of what will happen next.

Some people that don't know the PI industry speculate that it takes luck to catch people doing things that they aren't supposed to. But it's not luck. It's being prepared to succeed through preparation and persistence. Without a sincere commitment to the case, you can't be routinely successful. And any time you are running a business, you need to know what procedures will bear the highest potential for results. When I first started out, although my client may have given me a budget of eight hours, I may have spent twelve hours getting the results that I was happy with. It's not unusual to spend more time on a case or to, in hindsight, realize that there was an easier way. I won't hesitate to cut my bill back to make it seem things ran smoothly and without difficulty. I never let my client see or think that I struggled with a case. This in turn makes me look like a superhero. For me, in this profession, being a PI means that I have this special ability to solve problems or do things that others can't. And being a good PI means upholding this image.

MY IDENTITY

From age fourteen, I grew up bagging groceries and slicing lunch meat until I could learn how to "break down" a side of beef, cutting steaks and roasts. Working in retail at such an early age can have one of two outcomes: it can make you hate dealing with the public, or, as they say, it can "build character." The patrons in our store lived within the community we served. They shopped in our store week in and week out. The women in the store would introduce their daughters to me; they trusted me.

The store was not just a family business, it was a family. Even people that worked there who were not my relatives were still treated like family. The experience over the eight years that I worked there taught me that the client is always right, and that business is about building relationships. It wasn't easy, especially as I got older and eventually took over my grandfather's store in downtown Phoenixville. When I arrived at 7:00 a.m., I would immediately start grinding meat for hamburger. I then pulled large pieces of meat from the cooler and started cutting steaks, roasts, and pork chops. All of these items would be nicely displayed in my two glass cases where self-service was not an option. People took numbers, and personal service was given from start to finish. The same person that waited on them cut their lunch meat, pulled their steaks from the case, checked them out at the register, and bagged their groceries. And what I remember perhaps most vividly is that every day when I opened at 8:00 a.m., there was a line of people outside waiting to get in. That line represented satisfied repeat customers, just like my future insurance company accounts.

This early training helped form my traditional sense of business. But I had a lot of untraditional training as well. As a PI you never know what your next case will be. You don't know where it may be located or what you may need to do to get results. For people who like structure in their life—want an eight-to-five job or a specific set of job duties—you need to steer clear of being a PI.

I've always had an adventurous personality, combined with my somewhat ADHD tendencies. I enjoy having many different activities going on at one time so that I can jump from one activity to the next. In high school, our eleventh-grade class trip was to the Philadelphia Mint. But somehow when we arrived downtown, I encouraged six students to slip out of line and take the commuter train over the Ben Franklin Bridge to Camden. There we pretended to be eighteen and got so drunk we had to take a train all the way back home because we missed the field trip bus back to school.

On many occasions I was bored with school. I was heavily involved in sports, and growing up in the mid '70s, drug experimentation was also prevalent around me. I had friends that were not just athletes, but there were also those who were into fast cars and heavy partying. I had a diverse group of friends, grouped by titles like jocks, motorheads, and dopeheads. It wasn't unusual for me to skip school to have a house party somewhere or to go to the shore. One day, a group of us went to a house party and topped off our afternoon with a game of basketball at the elementary school I attended growing up, just five miles away from my high school. As a student athlete, it's not that I wasn't recognized by the teachers at the elementary school. When I made my way back to school, I immediately heard Principal Murphy's voice on the intercom, asking me to come to his office. Principal Murphy and I had a complex relationship. At first it was hostile, but that changed over time. At first, lectures, detention, and even suspension were used, but when I wasn't in school, I went to work at the meat market and would make money for the weekend. I also never denied anything I did when I talked to Principal Murphy, which must have made him mad, but it also built respect between us. I might not have given him every detail, but I admitted to being wrong. Eventually, Principal Murphy and I started to have "meetings," not disciplinary scolding. He would often be smoking in his office, and I remember on one occasion that he even offered me a cigarette. I was apparently tired of class and had backed my Chevy Nova onto the lawn at the entrance of the school. We had a large statue of our school mascot, the "Wildcat," at the entrance to our school, where students would sit in the sun on a nice day during their lunch break. I had opened my hatchback and propped up my twelve- by twenty-four-inch box speakers, so they were pointed toward the steps to liven up the sunning with some music. I guess someone reported that I had been there more than one period. On another occasion, we met to discuss my need to stick to a tighter attendance schedule after Principal Murphy advised me that I had missed twenty-six days in one marking period. His approach eventually worked, and we gained a mutual respect for each other.

My experiences in life enabled me to feel confident about knowing how to relate to people. Being able to hold a person's attention or invoke a sense of cooperation is crucial to being an investigator. The PI doesn't have a badge of authority to make anyone do anything. We need to be able to rely on our interpersonal skills. I always approach an interview or in-field contact, thinking that blending-in and making them think I'm one of them or perhaps even less fortunate than they are all means to getting people to willingly provide information. I have heard of instances where the police or an overbearing PI have tried to use their credentials to get information, and the witness simply says that he or she doesn't know anything, and the investigator walks away without any information. Conversely, a humble, friendly PI who approaches the house under the pretext that he or she is thinking about moving into the neighborhood usually has a better chance of getting the needed information. I have had a woman at the door tell me to hold on while she turns down the heat on her stove, and then she invites me into the house for a soft drink and to talk. This could have been the same woman that told the obtrusive investigator that she didn't know anything, and that she was busy cooking dinner. Your approach and how people perceive you are vital to your success at information gathering.

I worked a few months with a decorated marine right out of the service. He seemed to be the perfect candidate: disciplined, willing to get dirty, young, and smart. After three months he came into my office and said, "I'm going to resign." I asked why, and he said that he works all day, sitting surveillance, and when he goes to a person's door to gather more information, the first word out of his mouth is a *lie*. People see actions differently, and what I considered a necessary part of the job, this individual saw as a compromise of his integrity. He eventually went back into the Marine Corps and is a career serviceman.

It wasn't until much later in my career, when I started to train other investigators, that I realized what a huge advantage my upbringing made. I was a streetwise investigator. I had done and had experienced so many things that I could usually relate to the people or type of case I was working. You know how they say that you need to think like a criminal to catch a criminal? It wasn't that far of a stretch for me. And while this is not the confessions of a PI, I do and have skirted the edge of legal issues and actions. I will even admit to some minor transgressions, but I will contend that they were character building.

In 1980, the World's Fair was in Knoxville, Tennessee. Three friends and I decided that we were going to take Andy's VW bus on a road trip. That summer I had been a police officer at the shore. They endearingly referred to me as a summer rent-a-cop. This was the same summer that my partner Steve and I had a fifty-dollar bet to see who could hook up with more girls in one month. This annoyed some of our other associates, but we didn't take ourselves very seriously. We often covered for each other while one was skinny-dipping or under the boardwalk. When the station dispatch asked for an officer to respond to a complaint for a loud party, Steve and I would try to be the first responders. We wanted to find out where the best parties were for when our shift ended. During our trip to Knoxville one of our crew had his father's credit card, so we used that card to purchase not only gas but food and anything else they sold at the gas station convenience store. There were no computerized credit card transaction machines back then. If the card stated that it expired on 12/2013, it was good till then. Many places were supposed to ask for your driver's license number or car tag information, but apparently they never did. While initially distracted by the excitement of the road trip, I finally figured out that the card was not the guy's parents as he was doing everything he could to prevent our car tag from being seen. He was the only one that could make the payment and would purposely direct us to park on the opposite side of the gas pumps, obscuring our vehicle from direct site and using the most distant pump to make sure that our tag was not facing the station. The card was a major gas company card, which had been found on the boardwalk at the beach. We had used that card from Pennsylvania to Tennessee and not only bought gas, but food, drinks, and anything else we could charge from the convenience store, including fireworks and beer. Andy and I put a stop to the use of the stolen card. Unfortunately, I had been involved in my first fraud case but it opened my eyes to the ease of such a scheme.

When I returned from my trip, I went back to the police department to finish out the summer. While policing was fun, it just didn't raise my interest enough to want to make it my career. It didn't have the money I wanted to make or the type of work I wanted to do. I didn't have the personality or take myself seriously enough to work day-in and day-out as a police officer. And one might say that I had a character flaw: I was a risk taker and tended to brush off my actions or perhaps not think so seriously about the consequences. There were ten police interns that summer, and I wrote the least number of tickets out of everyone—not good for a business that relies on tickets as a source of funding. But ironically, I was the only intern offered a full-time position. However, I never lost sight of wanting to be an investigator.

BAD OFFICER, NO DOUGHNUT

I had a house in Bartow, Florida, that I purchased for an investment. I was in the process of fixing it up, but it was taking me longer than it should have. There were times when I wouldn't go to work on the house for weeks at a time. After one of these extended lapses, I went to the house to find that I had some visitors. The back door was broken into, and one of the back bedrooms was full of about one hundred DVDs and cellular phone accessories. All the items were new, and it was clear to me that they were most likely stolen items. I spoke to several neighbors, who stated that they had seen two men leaving the house in the morning, going out the back. I guess they never thought it was odd enough that the subjects never used the front door, to call the police. The items inside the house—sleeping bags and some duffel bags—suggested that the people were most likely transient.

This is where it gets interesting. I called the local sheriff's department and reported the matter and was told that an officer would get in touch with me. Within a few minutes, I was called by another sheriff's officer, who, after our conversation, reported that a break-in had occurred at a local store in the area. The description of the theft seemed to match the items in my house. I told the officer that if he came and watched the house, it appeared that the perpetrators would be back as their belongings were also present. He let out a little smirk and said, "How will I know when they will be back? Ask the neighbors to call the office when they see the guys again."

Around the same time, I saw a male in his late twenties pass by the street, and then I saw him again at an angle through a nearby path that the residents use to cut between the houses to a nearby convenience store. He was again looking in my direction. I waved to the subject to come here, and he made his way over. It was my gut feeling that he was involved some way in the DVDs ending up in my rental, so I just said, "Listen I'm going to put everything in the driveway. I'm not going to take any of your stuff—just stay out of my house." Needless to say, I put all the stuff in the driveway when I left, and when I came back the next day, everything was gone. Furthermore, I have had no further problems with any break-ins. The officer never called me back and never came to the neighborhood or talked to any of the neighbors. This case went unsolved and remains unsolved today. How many of you could have solved this case? Show up in a discreet vehicle, sit, and wait until the subjects return to the house.

There are no shortcuts to many investigations. Nor are most investigations too complex or too technical in nature for the average motivated person to be successful. The most significant factor is finding an investigator who will dedicate himself or herself and put in the time necessary. Sometimes this is regardless of what he or she is being paid. The PI industry as a whole left a big door open to newcomers like me. Many PIs in the past came from the law enforcement industry; many were retired officers and detectives. I have met many such investigators who feel that their time is worth more than an evolving industry will support. Like the sheriff's officer in the DVD theft case, their time is too important to waste sitting. I have had similar experiences with retired LEOs who went into the PI industry after a long, successful career in law enforcement. They completely misunderstand the amount of work that goes into the job, and their attempt at an investigations business is, at best, a hobby.

Just recently I was working a medical malpractice case in Naples. In this case I am working for a doctor who is being sued for alleged medical malpractice. The patient had a surgical procedure that he claimed made him worse or that resulted in another permanent injury. In these cases, I need to learn if the patient works anywhere. What are his duties at work? This subject claimed that the doctor caused some added permanent injury to his shoulder. But, after a few hours, I found out that the subject works for a landscaping company and followed him all day as he cut lawns, trimmed hedges, weeded, edged, and carried debris. This type of video can be used in the doctor's defense as he fights the suit. The video I secure, along with a well-written detailed report, will be sent to the attorney representing the doctor. If the case proceeds to trial, I will appear on behalf of the doctor in his defense and testify as to my work in the case, and the video evidence secured will be shown.

On another similar case, I was watching a subject who lived in a newer, middle-income neighborhood in Cape Coral, Florida. There were no trees in the community, and after the housing crash, several vacant homes were scattered throughout the subdivision. It was a really "easy sit," as we say in the industry, meaning that I could somewhat relax, sit in the front seat of my car parked in the driveway of a vacant home facing the garage door, and remain somewhat unnoticed. The house where I was sitting was on a corner lot, so from my position, I could see my target's home about ten houses away. I wasn't concerned with any of the neighbors, except the one directly behind me. No one could even see me or tell that I was in my car. I really didn't care about the guy behind me either because he would never know what house I was watching. I spent three days coming and going, and finally at one point the neighbor behind me, who I never tried to hide from, approached me and asked if I was a PI, and I said yes. He said that he was a retired cop and had also gotten his PI license a few years back, but that there was "just no money in the business." His house was nice, but he clearly felt he had made it in life, which is all relative to where you came from. He went on to tell me that he just couldn't understand why I would just sit in my car in the hot sun. He said that I should put up remote cameras and not waste my time sitting in the car. He acted as if I didn't know how to do my job. I am happy to report that I sometimes look younger than I am. Sometimes this plays to my advantage; other times, people think it's a weakness. But I politely told him that I usually get the best video of people after they leave their house, and in my opinion, there are no shortcuts to getting results. He didn't believe me and walked away with the same unfounded arrogance. This was not the first time—nor will it probably be the last—that an LEO would attempt to tell me how to do my job. Sometimes I will politely tell them that I would never approach their patrol car and try to tell them how to do their job. I usually follow this statement by saying, "I can assure you that I have been doing this long enough to know that this is the best approach."

A FALSE SENSE OF SECURITY

Our job is to access any neighborhood, subdivision, trailer park, high-rise, or location to successfully complete our investigation. There should be very few places we can't get into with a little ingenuity. I worked a case where I needed to track down a guy that stole millions of dollars from investors. He owned a home in Miami, but after a divorce, his wife took over the property. All of his mail continued to go to the ex's address, and while he wasn't staying there, she obviously knew how to get a hold of him but wasn't telling. According to the attorneys involved, they figured that her help might end the reported $20,000 a month she was getting from him in alimony. Much of my time on this case was spent searching public records. It's tough to exist in today's society without leaving paper trails that can be followed. After all, we are not looking for the Bin Ladens of the world; we are looking for regular working-class people most of the time. I was working for the investors who were swindled, and the goal was to find him and ascertain his assets. He was known to be a yachtsman and even owned a yacht brokerage business at one time. The feeling was that he was living on a yacht, and while he could be anywhere in the world, it was strongly believed that he was somewhere in South Florida.

When you search records on people, you also pay attention to information about other family members. I soon honed in on a condominium under his 82 year old mother's name found within the Boca Yacht and Tennis Club. This complex was located on the Intracoastal Waterway, directly across the street from the beach in Boca Raton. PIs have many ploys to get into guarded and gated facilities. If the community has a golf course, you can often say that you need to go to the clubhouse to inquire about private golf lessons. This is better than just saying that you are there to play golf because the club may be private, but few golf pros will turn down the request to meet to discuss private lessons. Another strategy is to look for a residence for sale and ask to meet a realtor there. Every case may be different, so there is no magic pill for all communities. If you are working on the fly and don't know the layout, your resourcefulness will never be under challenged, but you must get in!

With the Yacht Club so close to the beach, I saw residents walking in and out using a walking path. So I parked my car down the road, put on a hat, picked up a newspaper, and walked back right through security, using the pedestrian gate. Once inside, I investigated my surroundings, and there were definitely many livable yachts in the marina. However, I knew that I needed my car inside in order to stake out a building and didn't know how long it would take. My car provided the needed cover for an extended sit, so getting inside the compound was imperative.

I found that the building for the condominium I wanted to watch had a locked entrance door. I queried the list of names and units. I wrote down a random subject's name for my attempt to enter the building. I also found that by dialing zero on the keypad, I reached security at the front main gate. Often this is where the security runs its operations from in large communities. In a raspy voice, I stated the resident's name that I had jotted down from the building directory and told the gate attendant that I was going to meet a young man named John Bilyk. I asked that when he arrived to please direct him to the pool restaurant for our lunch meeting together. The security officer took down the guest's name, and I exited on foot. I returned fifteen minutes later with my license already out of my pocket and in my hand, hanging out the window. As I approached the gate, I handed it to the guard, stating that I was a visitor. He advised me to go to the clubhouse pool to meet my party and handed me a visitor's pass. Being able to get to where you need to be is often half the battle. People hide behind post office box addresses, gated communities, and falsified documents. Piercing these veils enables us to thoroughly work and get results.

Any time you arrive at a gated community, look for a resident's entrance that may be unstaffed before trying to use a pretext to get through the main manned entrance. When you pull up to the electronic keypad, look for the worn keys that may suggest a common code used by all residents.

Look at the inserted picture of the keypad for a condominium complex. Can you see the worn or dirty keys down the center of the key pad? Do you see that the code is "2580". When it's not as obvious as the above example, I try entering several common PIN codes, such as: 911, 123, 1234. Don't forget to enter the # sign if the directions call for its use before or after the number.

Some electronic gates are activated by a bar code on the side of the resident's vehicle. Others are activated by keypad or an electronic key card that the resident flashes in front of a sensor that activates the gate to open.

You may find that the only way to get into the subdivision will be to tailgate a resident through the gate. You may see signs advising that the gate will only allow one

car at a time. However cars are different lengths and a car or truck pulling a small trailer would need some variance. So whether it is a trailer or a tailgating car, a sensor will restrict the gate from closing when an obstacle is still present. You just need to stay close to the subject you're tailgating in behind. If the gate is a key card, I will have a similar looking white plastic card in my hand and act as if I am swiping it as I drive impatiently close to the resident in front of me. The picture of the double security gate consists of an arm and a metal gate. This is the entrance to a very secure high-rise with underground parking on a newly built condominium.

I took this second picture while I was inside the garage, identifying my subject's car and his mistress as they headed out to eat on Valentine's Day.

Despite the double-gated parking garage and signage stating that the gate would allow only one car at a time, I could tailgate a tenant into the complex. I had to obtain this position to identify the subject's car and be in position to properly conduct my surveillance.

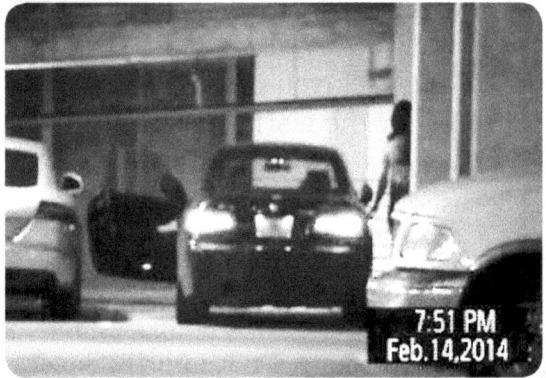

7:51 PM
Feb.14,2014

IT'S NOT BRAIN SURGERY

n July of 2013, I was given an assignment that was previously worked by another PI. The attorney told me that it was doubtful I would find the target. His paper trail would include a girlfriend's name and addresses from Naples to Hialeah, Florida. I thoroughly read through the prior investigator's ten page report, which I would only consider a lackluster effort. He touched on many leads but thoroughly worked none of them. He went running around the state haphazardly, only partially following up on each source or lead. I was in Miami at the time and started with the shabby mobile home park address where I found one of the subject's ex-girlfriends. The subject had lived with her over three years earlier, but after sitting and shooting the breeze, I found that she still had his phone number in her cellular phone directory. Getting the telephone number was a good lead, but that didn't mean that it would lead to the subject's address. I left on good terms and didn't disclose why I was looking for her old boyfriend (she never asked). I also got her number though, as a backup, in case I couldn't get the target to tell me his location. I figured that if I failed, I would pay her to try. I would willingly pay her twenty to forty dollars to call him and ask for an address if my attempt didn't work. Getting the payment I made to her could easily be billed to a client at three times the amount.

As a PI you need to collect sources, and for computer-related information, I call Cliff. Cliff was one of my interns, who, while wanting to be a PI, was already an accomplished computer science guru. Cliff has quite a history: with two undergraduate degrees and a master's in computer science. He loved to learn and enrolled in a local university, where he continued to surmount over 268 additional credits in four other disciplines. He took, and passed, the MCAT, GMAT, and LSAT, and while a Dean's list student, he was recently advised that if he didn't pick a major and graduate, he would be kicked out of school! They explained that by him not graduating from their university, he was adversely affecting their graduation rates. Cliff is about eight classes short of three more majors, including criminology, which he planned to complete.

Before calling Mr. Vasquez, I asked Cliff to check out the phone number I had. It's just not that difficult for a guy with this much know-how. Within a half hour, Cliff reported that the phone was still in working order and listed under our subject's name. He said that it was a "pay-as-you-go" phone with no contracts and, therefore, no billing address. However, he checked the service provider's records, and all calls to that number were going through the Okeechobee Road and Third Street tower in Hialeah. Now Cliff being Cliff proposed several options: one of them was something about sending a text message with an embedded executable file, but I said, "Let's wait till I call him first."

I had several addresses in Hialeah, and with his phone's signal using the Hialeah tower, it was apparent that he was still in the area. I also knew that he had an upcoming hearing, and that's why there was such a rush on me finding him. It was an important case; this was a guy who had been run over by a truck while riding his bicycle and was claiming to have suffered brain damage. When Cliff advised that his telephone number was still good, I was somewhat surprised. So I took the obvious next step: I called Mr. Vasquez and said, "Mr. Vasquez, this is John from Transportation Associates. I was advised that you have a hearing coming up, and I was asked to call you to see if you need transportation?" There are some things you can count on, and that's the fact that people taking advantage of the system won't turn down anything free. Mr. Vasquez was known to usually be intoxicated, and according to the police, he was intoxicated at the time of the accident. He had numerous DUIs and a suspended license, thus the reason that a bike was his main mode of transportation. It was also reported that he actually turned into the traffic and caused his own injuries because of being intoxicated. But this didn't stop him from suing the driver of the commercial truck. So after offering him a ride to the hearing, he immediately responded yes! I said, "What's your address?" He said, "I'm staying at the Executive Suite Motel, but I'm leaving here tonight to find another motel later today." I then asked, "What room are you in?" And he said, "208." I then immediately stated, "You know, I'll call you back on Thursday when you find the new location," and he said, "Okay." I quickly went to his hotel, stayed on him the rest of the day, followed him that night as he left on foot, and after he checked into the new hotel, I checked in behind him. For the next three days I shadowed him everywhere he went and secured more than three hours of video of him walking, visiting friends, going to eat, buying beer and wine for a party in his room, and acting, as best defined, as a guy without any real agenda.

You can't be tentative about taking the next step or sounding uncertain about yourself while delivering a pretext. You must be convincing, confident, and determined to get the information you need.

HAPPY TRAILS

When we speak of paper trails, we mean traces of information that people leave behind as they move from one place to another. We continuously leave bits and pieces of information behind as clues to where we have been or what we may have done. For a "locate investigation," each time a person moves, there is an address added to his or her history and new sources of information to contact. Information left behind at one address may be more valuable than information left at another. You may have lived in one neighborhood where you and your neighbor had a particular bond, similar interest or hobby. You may have worked together, gone to the same high school, or may have been involved in a common activity. This person may know more about you than any other neighbor at any other address where you just didn't associate with anyone else. The more productive address will disclose leads that need to be followed up on, such as the identified high school, workplace, or softball team they both played on.

Like the saying "leave no rock unturned," we need to have the determination to pursue each lead thoroughly. I will go into very detailed steps later in this book under the chapter of "Locate Investigations," but you need to understand that whether on purpose or accidental we leave a trail as we proceed through life. People routinely query car insurance websites that prompt them to enter their address. Online car insurance premium quotes utilize some basic information to provide the inquirer with an immediate quote. This basic information is the age of the driver, the type of car, and the location of where the car is "garaged." So if I go to one of the national car insurance sites and put in the address of a person, I may find a list of the cars associated to that address. This is just an example of an unintentional paper trail and not necessarily a tool an investigator would rely on. We use fee-based companies that associate cars to addresses through the Department of Motor Vehicle tag registration information.

The fact is that trails of information are unconsciously left behind all the time. In this electronic age, we leave trails all over the place, like: when we buy a home; get married or divorced; fill out an apartment rental agreement; submit a job application; complete an electric service agreement; request household gas company service; obtain cable or a cell phone service or a hunting license, fishing license, occupational or professional license, or driver's license; have an arrest record; file a civil suit; get a speeding ticket, parking ticket, or even an e-pass sensor for paying tolls.

As the sources of potential information increase, access to the information becomes easier as it is tethered to digital files and databases. Dropping off the "grid" is not as easy as it used to be, and many locates are done from a computer as your unavoidable electronic footprint is easy to track.

DATABASES AND RECORD SEARCHES

Before the Internet or even a very powerful workplace computer, research was done in person, at the courthouse, or over the phone. If you were doing a locate investigation, you could expect to spend hours in the courthouse reviewing property records, tax rolls, voters' registration cards, hunting, fishing and driver's license information, as well as driving records, vehicle registrations, parking tickets, and criminal records. This meant time in the field, gas, and miles on your vehicle. Many investigation firms also had an account or access to reports from a major credit reporting agency. The accounts were usually set up in a "merchant" business name. This enabled access to a person's credit report and "identifying information," social security number, date of birth, address, and perhaps employer. It also identified his or her "trade lines," which were the businesses the person had lines of credit with, along with the names of the creditors, the account numbers, and contact numbers for the creditors. These reports were like gold; they contained a ton of information useful for working a locate investigation over the phone. Collection agencies and skip tracers had been using these same methods for years, tracking down people who "skipped out" or failed to repay a loan and left their former address.

So if my target had a Burdines Department Store credit card, it wasn't uncommon for me to call Burdines and ask for the collections department. I would get a person accustomed to doing collection work over the phone, and I would merely act as another merchant's agent doing the same job. I would read information off the credit report, which would legitimize who I was or who I alleged to be and would advise that I was trying to find our account holder. Without going into too much detail, I would ask if the subject possibly recently reported a change of address. After all, it's not uncommon for someone to call the store or business that they have a store credit card with and notify them first of their move and new address. Keep in mind that businesses may only report information to the credit agency periodically or monthly when payment histories are reported and balances change. So the information we got from the merchant, bank, or lender was usually the most updated information possible before going into the field. And once I built up a rapport with the merchant, I would go on to ask them if they had any employer information or co-applicant on file.

The blossoming of the Internet in the 1990s brought online record search access. Information that had only been available at the courthouse could suddenly be accessed online. The department of motor vehicles (DMV) started to release its information in digital format, either directly accessible with a direct user account or through a third party. The only problem was that you had to search the Internet for all the different sites and sources to find bits and pieces of information. And, the true Holy Grail of information was still the subject's most up-to-date address history. This information could still only be obtained from one of the three major credit reporting agencies: Experian, Trans Union, or Equifax.

This would all change when a man named Hank Asher created a computer-generated comprehensive report that would not only data mine all the public sources of information but would also contain information from a credit reporting agency known as the "credit header." This information included the subject's identifying information: name, address history, SSN, and date of birth. This enabled us to verify the subject's spelling of his or her name; confirm that the name was valid by the linked SSN, and, of course, get the most reliable current and former address history information. The address provided was where the subject had his or her bills sent. It was the address that he or she put on applications, apartment rentals, car loans, or mortgages. We didn't need the merchant account information, the credit scores, or payment history; we just needed the address and enough other identifying information to confirm that we were tracking the right person. Hank Asher delivered that product and as a result of his work is considered a legend in the investigative community.

In 1992, Hank Asher started a business called Database Technologies (DBT), which provided the investigator with the first comprehensive report.

In 1999, DBT Online bought Asher out for $147 million after the FBI and the Drug Enforcement Administration suspended their contracts, following revelations that in 1982, Asher was involved in drug dealings while he was living in the Bahamas. The DEA reported concerns that the company could potentially monitor targets of their investigations.

In 2000, Choice Point, an Equifax company, bought DBT for $462 million dollars and won many government contracts back.

Choice Point would later suffer several security breaches, which led to the theft of personal information, which facilitated a reported 750 cases of identity theft. The scam came to light when a forty-one-year-old Nigerian citizen, Olatunji Oluwatosin, was arrested in October 2004 with five cell phones and three credit cards that belonged to other people. The substantial breach in 2004 led to a $10 million class-action settlement and called for new national privacy laws in the United States to protect the personal data of Americans.

In 2008, Lexis Nexis bought Choice Point for $775 million dollars.

In 2011, Mr. Asher returned to the industry he originally created and formed a new company, called "TLO." He boasted that TLO created a faster, more accurate, and more thorough database report—better than any of his previous products.

In January 2013, the "father of data fusion," Hank Asher died, and TLO went into Bankruptcy.

In December 2013, TLO was purchased by Trans Union for around $166 million and launched Hank's database report, called TLOxp, which is touted to be the "most powerful database for background research on people, assets, and businesses." TLOxp is reportedly designed to get you the exact information, even in cases where you only have partial source data, such as an incomplete SSN or address. It is also possible to search for a subject using a phonetic name spelling, location radius, or age range.

According to the *South Florida Business Journal* Lexis Nexis was also interested and prepared to offer $180 million, but it was too late as Trans Union's offer had already been approved.

If you go on the Internet, you will find dozens of companies offering up people searches for a fee. You probably never heard of TLO or Lexis Nexis, but in the PI's world these are the primary database powerhouses with dependable, verified sourced information. Keep in mind that an account with either of these two companies will require significant vetting, verification of licenses, training requirements, and possibly a site visit.

If I were going to do a background check on a subject, I would consider all the "source data" that I had available to me. Some investigators may have (private) sources that others don't have, but let's consider what is readily available.

In Florida, I can go to the Florida Department of Law Enforcement (FDLE) website, and for twenty-five dollars, buy an immediate statewide criminal history check for any subject. Most other states also have similar statewide agency sites that sell this collected information to the public. I can also get a seven- or twelve-year driving record from the county courthouse traffic division.

I can run my TLO or Lexis Nexis report and get: your SSN, DOB, address, cellular phone number and carrier, your property ownership records, address history for about twenty years, vehicle registration records and driver's license number, name address, type, issue date, and height (no picture). Depending on your age, your SSN will tell me what state you were born in or perhaps where you came of age to start working. Also depending on your age, if I look far enough back in your address history and it matches with your SSN, I will probably determine the house you grew up in. An address search of just that house address should show me other people with your same last name who used that address. These people would be your parents and any siblings. Separate searches could be done on each one of those names to determine where they are today, in case I need to speak to them to find you.

I can go online in the county where you live or, based on your address history, all the counties you previous lived in and search online civil and criminal records in each county. This will tell me if you have ever been involved in a civil suit either as the plaintiff or defendant in those regions. Have you ever sued anyone or been sued? Is there a criminal arrest in which you were not charged or convicted and, therefore, is not on your statewide criminal record? I can check each police department in each town where you lived and search for any incident reports under your name. I can also search for any incidents that occurred at your address and determine the nature of the incident, what people were involved, and whether there is a separate report under another name.

I can go online and check workers' compensation claim records to see if you have ever been hurt on the job, the nature of your injury, and how long you were off from work.

I will check county property records to determine the value, size and location of the house you live in. If you don't own it, I will determine who your landlord and property owner is by the tax bill receipt. This will also give me their mailing addresses, and if I need more information, I can refer to my TLO database account and most likely get a phone number for your landlord. If you owned the house, I will look at your tax payment history to see if you had problems paying your taxes and if a tax certificate was ever issued. I will look at the value you paid for your house versus what it is worth right now to determine if you are underwater or have a gain. I will look at the houses you owned and sold in the past to judge your possible wealth and financial situation. By the documentary stamp tax on the deed, I can determine the purchase price of the property and deduct your recorded mortgage amount to determine how much was put down in cash.

I can use Google Earth and conduct a street view to possibly see an image of your house, which may include the cars in your driveway, boat in the back, camper, or RV. An image solely of your house may also be available during my perusal of the County Property Appraisers Office's records. I can check building and zoning records to see if there has been any contractor's work done on your house where a permit was pulled. The contractor listed could possibly be you, the homeowner, indicating that the work was done by you. If subcontractors are listed, and you, the homeowner, were acting as the general contractor, then the subs most likely interacted with you and may have information pertinent to my investigation.

I'll go on Facebook for an ID picture of you or check Twitter and other social media sites to see if you have any uploaded content I can use to form my assessment.

I can contact your neighbors, employer, work associates, references, and relatives.

Based on the information I was able to gather—the type of car you drive, the house you live in, your employment, home rental or real estate purchase transactions, criminal, civil, and social media information, and personal interviews—you would be surprised to see how close of a personal profile I can generate that tells a lot about you.

The above search I outlined is very typical of a background investigation. I have conducted these types of searches for business partners, insurance companies, landlords, employers, and attorneys. I have even been provided jurors' names to research so that counsel has a better understanding of the jury.

Over the years, PIs develop contacts that become vitally important to their work. A friend who works at a hotel reservation desk can be helpful in identifying a room number or reservation date for a case. If your town has a large taxi company, a source there can tell you where people are picked up and dropped off. So building business relationships is vital, and protecting your sources is equally important. I wouldn't put the name of the taxi company or even how I obtained the information in my report. The best investigator will have many sources and know how to access different types of information.

MY OWN DATA MINING

My understanding of exposing and following paper trails has served me well over the years, not only on cases I was paid to investigate but also in building my own personal wealth. Early in my career, I realized the importance of information and knowing how to find it and use it. I think between the research and pressure to get results, your work ethic doesn't allow you to overlook an opportunity. I have always been competitive, and I have a drive to always do something more. What I have done so far is never good enough, and I need to do more or find something else to accomplish. I don't think we can instill that same motivation if we just praise kids at all levels, regardless of their performance. Some people contend that kids will do well as long as they have a strong sense of confidence, but I can see this leading to complacency. To me it's similar to those that feel they are entitled to free services or assistance. How can you be hungry for something if you feel you're entitled to it or if it comes to you without effort?

Being around the courthouse doing research made me keen on how real estate transactions are recorded and the various stages or actions taken with property. For instance, if I saw a transaction of a property using a Quit Claim Deed, I knew by the very nature of the instrument that this was most likely a property transferred between family, friends, or associates. A Lis Pendis filing signified the onset of a mortgage foreclosure. A Tax Deed Certificate meant that the property owner was unable or unwilling to pay his or her property taxes. So if I wanted to, I could contact these individuals to see if there was any possible business solution that could benefit both of us. Let's say that you owned your home for ten years and lost your job, and the bank was foreclosing on your property. Maybe at best, if you sold it, you would break even, but then you would have nothing. You may be ready to walk away because you need to start over again somewhere else, perhaps another city. It could be that five thousand dollars would provide the homeowner with enough money for a new start. Or perhaps this payment is for a business agreement where the owner stays in the property as a tenant and agrees to sell the house later when the real estate market improves and then split the profit with the investor.

You never know the possibilities until you identify these types of situations, and knowing how to find the properties is the first step.

For about two months, I drove past a house that had a fallen tree lying on its roof as the result of the 2007 hurricanes which came through Central Florida. After noting the house to be vacant every time I drove by, I decided to research the property and found that the owner had passed away. The house had been empty for over a year, and he had no heirs. I found that the taxes were being paid by a local investor through a process known as buying tax certificates. Tax certificates are basically notes, offering investors the opportunity to earn an attractive rate of return for paying the property taxes of another individual or entity. When the property is sold, the investor recoups his or her money plus the interest he or she charged for paying the taxes. One way to force an owner to sell the house is to file a tax deed foreclosure. Once the investor has a tax certificate that is two years old, he or she can file for foreclosure. This doesn't mean that this individual automatically owns the property; it just means that the property is forced to a tax deed auction, unless the owner is able to repay the investor the taxes paid plus the attractive interest and costs associated with the foreclosure filing. If the owner does not come forth to settle the tax issue, then the house is sold to the highest bidder. The proceeds from the purchaser of the property are used by the county to pay the investor, and the surplus is returned to the original owner. Many times tax deed sales are less spoken about compared to regular foreclosures, and as a result, the attendance of those interested in buying tax deed foreclosed properties is not as competitive. And, if you where the one filing the foreclosure, chances are that you know more about the value of the house than anyone else, which puts you in a very key position.

With the house I pursued, the owner was deceased, so when it went to auction just two people were bidding: one other guy and I. The other guy had no real knowledge of the house, its condition, or its value. He was just playing in the process, and I ended up buying the property for $70,000, or about half of what the house was worth.

Had the owner of the property been alive, any surplus proceeds from the sale would have gone back to the owner. After the sale is completed, the county will mail out a written notice advising the original owner of any remaining surplus he or she is entitled to claim. The letter usually goes to the address on file, and they are not required to go out of their way to locate the prior owner. These surplus funds are held by the county for typically up to one year (varies from county to county) before they are barred from ever being able to be collected and revert to the county. Almost every county in Florida has a tax deed surplus list that investigators use to track down heirs and prior owners. This type of PI work is called "asset recovery," and anyone, any age, can partake in it. Here you can see investigator Zoe, who, after being in the real estate industry for over twenty years made her move to asset recovery investigations.

DIRTY LITTLE SECRETS

Sometimes the paper trail you create is left on the property while you are still there. Investigators routinely pull the trash when they see it placed out on the curb for collection. Other times, we plan the "trash pulls" as a designated objective for additional information gathering. When trash is the objective, I arrive around 5:00 a.m. or earlier, and if it is present, I immediately pull the trash and take it off-site to review. But sometimes a person may not put his or her trash out until the last minute. When I see a last-minute placement, I stop the trash truck right before they get to my subject's street and arrange to have the trash saved for me until we meet somewhere away from the target's residence. I always talk to the driver; he or she is the one in charge of the crew, and I tip him or her ten dollars. I have never had any driver refuse the offer. From my experience, I would gather that PIs are not the only ones requesting this service. When arranging the assistance of the collection crew, be specific in telling them the exact color and location of the can. When they "pull" the trash, tell them to raise the bags in the air so you can clearly ID the bag color, and if it's white, it helps to look for the color of the top drawstrings. They will throw it into the back of the truck but not initiate the compactor. Tell them that you will meet them down the street to retrieve the bags. I carry a couple of large black fifty-five-gallon plastic trash bags with me all the time so that they can drop the smaller bags inside my larger bag. I also carry a small box of disposable latex gloves for sorting through the debris after I am safely away from the area. Never underestimate the potential lead creator or even case breaker that may come from the trash.

Trash-pulls have worked in so many cases that I make it a practice to pull trash whenever possible on virtually every type of case. As hard as it may be to believe, the distributor of a bounce house, one of those air-filled party accessories, was sued by the parent of a child who attended a birthday party. The single mother claimed that her daughter hurt her arm while jumping up and down inside. According to the lawsuit, her thirteen-year-old daughter got her arm caught in the webbed walls of the bounce house. According to the mother, her arm was nearly ripped from the socket, and now she is in constant pain, can't play the violin anymore, and is doing poorly in school. Well, at least those were the allegations, and many plaintiff attorneys would jump at the opportunity to take this case. For me the case was a simple straightforward surveillance. I just needed to avoid being arrested or having the police called on me for stalking a little girl on the playground at her middle school. The case took an interesting twist when I followed the girl and her mother from their apartment building, and they stopped at the apartment complex's dumpster to throw out the trash.

I was surprised to see that the mother tossed three bags into the dumpster. I was planning on following them out of the area, but I couldn't afford to lose site of the trash. What if while I was out of the area, the trash collection truck came and emptied the dumpster? I knew that the mother was taking the girl to school, and I had plenty of time to do surveillance work at her school, so I stopped in my tracks to pull those discarded trash bags once the two left the complex. The amount of documents thrown away in one disposal was unusual. This trash-pull yielded many documents signaling that the mother, Ms. Linda McBride, was experiencing severe financial problems. I saw a Cobra document for insurance, which suggested that she may have lost her job. I also found many late notices from her car company, cable company, and apartment complex, all stating that she was behind in payments. Her apartment complex was also threatening eviction, and at one point her car had apparently been repossessed as a letter stated that her 2003 Chevrolet Tracker was scheduled to be sold at auction. Then there was the string of prescriptions from different doctors, all in the mother's name. She seemed to be "doctor shopping" until she found a doctor who would prescribe her the medication she wanted. Many prescriptions were thrown away unfilled but not the ones for Oxycodone. The letters accumulated showed a person in financial turmoil, but the dagger was a four-page handwritten letter from her incarcerated husband. According to the Department of Corrections (DOC) website's inmate records, her husband was sentenced to twenty years for drug solicitation (heroin). In his letter he calls the mother "unfit and a drug addict." If all of this wasn't bad enough, I also found computer printouts of the little girl's school transcripts, which showed that she did well while being in school, but when it came to homework, she had zeros on almost every assignment.

In total, the documents painted a disruptive and perhaps dysfunctional household. It's no doubt that the little girl, at thirteen, was aware of many of the financial problems her mom was facing as well as those associated with her mother's drug use. The added concern could be whether perhaps the little girl herself was abusing prescription pills, based on her mother and father's drug history.

From the information gained from a simple trash-pull, I found information that suggested that the girl's problem at school may not be related to an injury, if one even occurred.

When you pull the trash, park your car a couple of doors away from the target's house and leave a door, window, or trunk open to quickly throw the trash into your vehicle. Be aware of your surroundings, but don't look suspicious. Be deliberate in your movements: go directly to the trash can, open the lid, pull the bag, walk to your car immediately, and throw the bag inside.

I was hired to serve a summons and was appointed a "special process server" by the court for a specific case I worked. Process servers serve summonses, requiring defendants to come to court to answer a complaint filed by a plaintiff. Process servers also serve subpoenas on witnesses, requiring them to appear or provide information sought by the party issuing the subpoena. A summons is served on a person who is a party to the suit, not just a witness, so this can be a life-altering matter when someone is suing you. An attorney can motion the court to appoint a PI to serve papers on a case-by-case basis when a subject may be eluding a normal process server. In order for a PI to serve a summons, a judge must grant the motion to appoint a "special process server." Without this special appointment, only a licensed process server can serve a summons. On the other hand, a PI can serve a subpoena without any special appointment or license. In fact, anyone over the age of eighteen can serve a subpoena, so a PI has no special privileges when it comes to process service.

The serving or delivering of any legal notice regarding the progress or process of a case is referred to as process serving. The service or delivery of these notices is important and is a regulated activity. Licensed process servers have undergone specific educational training regarding the rules and procedures for service. They are licensed or appointed to serve process by designated counties. They are not statewide licensed, individual county or regional licenses are required to cover multiple counties. Most sheriffs' departments have deputies who serve process as part of their daily responsibilities. There are also private process servers who work for private companies.

There are important rules and regulations to obey when serving a subpoena or summons, and classes on process serving explain these rules and regulations to the applicant wanting to become a process server.

The typical charge to have a subpoena or summons served is usually under fifty dollars. Businesses performing this service usually do it on a high-volume basis to make the business practical. But at the same time, for fifty dollars, the "process server" cannot afford to spend a lot of time or expense on a service because of the inexpensive rates. On the other hand, a PI who has been hired and appointed as a special process server for a difficult witness may need to locate and track down a subject as part of the service. In these cases the hired PI may use various tactics, including surveillance. The PI will also bill out his or her time on an hourly basis, plus expenses.

I was contacted by an attorney who told me that he had been trying to serve a person who just happened to be an ex-attorney. He had already used three different process serving companies as well as the Sheriff's Department with no success. He decided to hire me at a greater expense since he needed the guy served in order to move forward with the case. I ran the typical database on my subject and knew his cars and his family members. While being out one night in the area, I swung by my next victim's house and noticed that the trash was out already. I pulled down the street and walked up to his can and pulled one bag of trash. On reviewing the trash, there was a Post-it note that said that Tommy's birthday party was Saturday, 2:00 p.m., at Pirates of the Caribbean miniature golf. Tommy was the subject's eight-year-old son. The next day, I called the miniature golf course and confirmed that the Saturday party was the next day. I showed up to serve Mr. Attorney as he unloaded his family and party supplies for the event. When I walked up to him and spoke his name, he responded, thinking that I was with the miniature golf course staff. I said, "This is for you," handed him the summons, and walked away.

I worked a case in Ft. Myers where the woman traveled between Puerto Rico and the States. We had several investigators appointed to serve the woman and spent several days trying to establish if she was in Puerto Rico or Ft. Myers. When the woman came to or left the house in Ft. Myers, she would always use her garage. In Puerto Rico she rarely left her high-rise, with secure parking underground. We never knew what car she was in or if and when she left.

We finally got a break when she was in Ft. Myers. The woman knew better than to answer the door for someone she didn't know. We sat surveillance on her house, verifying that she was there. We could have continued to sit, but I wanted to make her move on my own agenda. I had brought a small hand pump pest-control sprayer filled with water. I parked my car a couple of houses away and approached her house on foot. I sprayed the front of her house thoroughly until I knew that I caught her attention. I moved to the side and around back where, finally, I guess she couldn't resist confronting me about what I was doing. As I moved closer to her, I told her that we had been getting many calls about termites. Just as I was in the middle of a sentence and within arm's length of her, I pulled the summons from my back pocket and handed it to her. At the same time I held up my smartphone and took her picture as she was looking down at the court order to appear—assignment complete!

CASE CLOSED

You don't always know how a case will turn out or even how you will immediately proceed until you get started. You may need to make some personal visits to locations and talk to people in order to develop some leads to pursue or even ideas for what tactics to use. And most of all, there will usually never be any real notoriety or publicity for the cases you are working. The reality is that we handle common problems of ordinary people and businesses. We are resolution specialists and problem solvers, and we never know the type of case we will get one week from the next. I received a call from a condominium complex management office stating that a resident believed that his neighbor, whom he was feuding with, was defecating on his back porch. Each week he found fresh human waste on his patio, and he wanted to catch the guy or whoever was committing the indecent act. Ironically, it reminded me of my college wrestler roommate who liked to perform his own little indecent acts in the refrigerator vegetable compartments of our rival fraternity houses. Imagine opening the refrigerator the next morning and being hit with that unpleasant sight or, worse yet, having to be the one to clean it!

So once again my exposure and experiences made me a well-qualified candidate to tackle this unsolved mystery. I grew up in Pennsylvania, where deer hunting was a popular sport, and in some areas, the first day of deer season was an official school holiday. The weeks and months leading up to the opening day were filled with scouting the property for signs of deer tracks and presence. When you have a large tract of land, it's best to do your homework to know where the deer are running. To survey the activity on the property, we commonly use outdoor motion-detector cameras, specifically designed to be mounted on trees. The cameras come in weather-resistant boxes and work with SD memory cards and batteries. The batteries enable the camera to work for several weeks at a time. When the camera detects movement, it takes still pictures or video, depending on the setting of the camera. The cameras are activated by motion detectors, and in complete darkness, they have built-in flashes to illuminate the object. For a more stealth operation, the flash can be turned off as long as there is still some light available. The cameras are usually camouflage or dark green in color and hard to spot. These cameras are highly reliable and built of durable weatherized material. There are many different manufacturers and ranges of quality, with the average starting price of a medium-grade unit around eighty dollars. I mounted two of these cameras in the back of my customer's house, and in one week, we found Mr. Crapper, who, once confronted, stated that he was doing the midnight poop run because my client's dog was pinching them off in his yard.

I used these same cameras in a domestic infidelity case about a year back. My client came to me, reporting that she felt that her husband was cheating with his twenty-five-year-old marketing representative. My client noticed her fifty-year-old husband dressing in younger-styled hip clothing. He was a prominent businessperson in the community, and he managed and built airport hangars at an executive airport. While at work he would park in a hangar where his offices were located. When he would leave, his dark-tinted windows prevented anyone from seeing who was or wasn't in the car. His preferred love nest, when not suspected of a "quickie" in the car, was his Cocoa Beach condominium. The condominium was a perfect location because it had "under the building" parking, so he could drive from the hangar at work to the garage at the condominium without any risk of exposure. He was even brazen enough to change the locks on the condominium so that my client couldn't get me inside to install cameras. I traveled to the condominium and observed the garage parking under the building. The garage entrance was gated, but then there were also individual two-car garages inside. So the tenants pulled through the security gate, drove under the building, pushed their garage door openers, and then parked their car inside a private garage. They then exited the private garage and entered a small, locked lobby that housed the elevator to the residences. I took one of my inexpensive "deer tracking" motion-detector cameras and spray-painted it white to match the white walls inside the garage. I mounted the camera over the lobby door with a wedge angling it directly on the cheating spouse's garage. After two weeks I had over fifty pictures, six pictures of which proved my client's suspicions: he was bringing his little hottie to the blazing beach.

VARIETY, THE SPICE OF LIFE

Throughout my career I have conducted hundreds of different types of investigations that warranted me to jump in and work the case to see where it would take me. After working many cases, you start to recognize possible scenarios or similarities with cases and what may have happened. There are also those kinds of cases that involve something completely different that you have never done before. I can honestly say that I was educated through my line of work rather than bringing any technical education or experience to my job. It has been that unknown factor that has kept my job interesting and has enabled me to spend thirty years in the same industry.

In all cases, I learned to utilize research skills to look up information that I didn't know or didn't understand and there was a lot of that. My practice was focused on insurance claims and business liability issues. This is a good area of specialization because there will never be a shortage of people getting hurt or developing different schemes to make money. And the deep pockets of major businesses will always be targets of those looking for a big payout. We have come to a point where many people don't accept any responsibility for their actions and believe that someone else is always at fault. In the PI industry, we call this the victim syndrome.

I am going to break down some common investigations and the procedures used to work the case.

If someone slipped and fell in a supermarket, I would investigate what caused the fall. Could it have been prevented? What can be done to prevent a similar accident from occurring again, and was it a realistic or a legitimate accident? Was it possibly staged or exaggerated, and can I discover if there is an actual hazard that caused the incident? I first need to identify the specific location where the fall occurred. The location may be determined by an accident report, incident report, eyewitness, the injured party, the manager, or a worker who may have already determined this fact. I can then start to inquire whether more than just one person has randomly fallen in this specific area. I can't just rule out the possibility that the injured party didn't just trip on his or her own feet, had worn out slippery shoes, was wearing flip-flops or had untied shoelaces, or whether some other contributing factor caused the accident. When I conduct my investigation, I am going there to aggressively get answers. I can't come back and say that I don't know what happened.

When investigating an accident, you need to look for any ambiguity with the reporting or description of the accident. Proving or disproving the likeliness of the accident will take documentation. Is there any store video that shows the incident as it took place? If there is no sign of any standing hazard, gather facts and statistics that may also cast some doubt on the incident actually being a liable accident. Accidents occur all the time, but those that occur because of a problematic situation are those where liability arises; thus, damages may be brought against the property owner. With statistics, you may find that a store has over two hundred register receipts daily, and at a minimum this would mean that two hundred people may walk through the same door or over the same threshold that the one customer reportedly tripped over. You may photograph the threshold and find it flush and without any obstruction that could have contributed to the fall. Secondly, you might speak to or take statements from several patrons of the store in the parking lot after they have left the store. You may look for an elderly woman or one using a cane and try to get a quick statement from her, asking how many times a week she visits the store and for how many years she has been coming. You would then specifically ask her if she has ever tripped in the area of the accident location or if she has ever felt this area unsafe or a hazardous condition. Obviously you are hoping to hear, "I have been coming to this store for twenty- five years and have had a hip replacement and use a cane. I usually come to the store twice a week and exit through those doors each time, and I have never tripped or ever felt that the exit was dangerous or presented a hazard." You then ask if I can just take a quick picture, hold up your phone, and snap her picture. During the statement you would have also asked the woman her name and telephone number. By working the parking lot, you can see her walk to her car and get the tag to further identify her address.

The determination of whether the person slipped or tripped can also help defend the case.

I was contacted by a client and asked to conduct an accident scene investigation in South Florida. I was advised that a woman had slipped at the res-taurant and had hired an attorney. I contacted the restaurant and learned that an employee of the restaurant witnessed the fall, which occurred outside the restaurant. I arranged to meet with the witness and secure her statement as well as make general observa-tions of the area. I was also requested to contact the plaintiff's attorney and arrange to secure the injured woman's statement. During my first contact with her attorney, I was advised that the injured woman stated that she slipped on ice that had been dropped on the sidewalk by the restaurant staff. This restaurant used the sidewalk to service the outside patio area.

I called the restaurant and spoke to the manager, and he advised me that the witness, Ms. Mallory Snook, did not work until the following evening. I therefore arranged to meet Ms. Snook at the onset of her shift the following day. I arrived early at the restaurant to familiarize myself with the area and layout. I found that the restaurant has outdoor dining that is separated from the city sidewalk by a steel railing. The sidewalk outside the restaurant is used by the general public throughout the day, and there is another restaurant next door to the north on Ocean Drive. With such a busy public sidewalk, anyone could have spilled or dropped debris. It is also not under any cover and exposed to the elements. It is a typical city sidewalk, maintained by the city of Lauderdale by the Sea.

Ms. Snook arrived and agreed to provide a recorded statement. She has been a server for almost one year at Ocean Breeze. She recalled the incident and described the claimant as a portly female, about five feet six inches tall, and around 260 pounds. She felt that the woman looked younger than her reported fifty-five-year-old description. She stated that she had just dropped off some food at a table and was walking back to enter the restaurant when she saw the woman stumble. She saw the woman fall forward, scraping her right knee. She didn't recall what the woman was wearing but knew that her knees were exposed. The witness took me outside and pinpointed the exact location of the fall on the city sidewalk just outside the restaurant. She did not believe that the plaintiff had eaten in the restaurant, but that she was just walking by. When she asked the injured woman if she was okay, she said yes but appeared a little embarrassed. The woman never mentioned anything about water or melted ice on the ground, and the server did not recall seeing anything on the sidewalk that could have caused the woman to fall. The witness took me outside to the area directly east of the outside tables. This sidewalk is used by the general public, and the restaurant area is separated by a banister. As I walked the sidewalk, I noticed that the ground seemed uneven. The cement was a rolling surface and not completely flat. It's not discernable from the eye, but laying a straight edge on the ground shows areas of unevenness.

As I walked the area, I could feel how someone could have stubbed a shoe, causing him or her to fall forward. Since most slips occur backward, it is more likely that she tripped as opposed to slipped. As indicated, I could feel the rolling sidewalk beneath my shoes, and having worked many trip-and-fall cases it's something I look for immediately. The cause now seemed more obvious to me. A picture taken in the precise area of the fall on the city sidewalk showed two distinct dips: one in the middle and one to the right of the four-foot straight edge. The shadowed areas in the middle and to the right show dips of approximately one-quarter of an inch in the sidewalk. The rolling pavement is easily an area where a shoe can be caught and cause a trip.

You can find many studies about accidents conducted by various safety groups. I started thinking about the subject falling forward onto her knee and realized that this could not have been a slip. Most studies show that a "slip" occurs when there is too little traction or friction between the shoe and the walking surface. A "trip" occurs when a person's foot contacts an object in his or her way or drops to a lower level unexpectedly, causing him or her to be thrown off-balance. *A trip most often results in a person falling forward, while a slip most often results in the person falling backward. A "fall" occurs when you are too far off-balance.*

Most slip, trip, and fall incidents are preventable with general precautions and safety measures. Many falls occur in the areas of curbs, flaws in parking lots, and uneven surfaces. None of the objects or surfaces are of a significant height but they still have the potential to cause significant injuries. The best way to prevent injuries such as these is to be aware of where you are going and pay attention to your walking surface. When I have the opportunity to speak to the injured party, I always ask him or her what he or she was doing at the time of the incident. In this case, she was walking and talking to a male subject that she had met downtown, and they were deciding where to go eat. I also learned that she was overweight, and another point of interest that may be relative is that heavier people tend not to lift their feet high off the ground. Some shuffle their feet rather than lifting them cleanly off the ground. This sometimes causes more contact with surfaces and makes them more likely to trip on an uneven or cracked surface.

Thinking on your feet about how to approach an investigation will vary from case to case and becomes easier overtime. You have heard me say many times that the investigator has to use his or her imagination, and this is often how we come up with the possible scenarios of how an accident may have occurred when the evidence is incomplete. It is then up to the investigator to check out whether the available evidence can support this possible causation.

I was assigned a case where a hotel guest stated that the shower head shot off and hit him in the head while he was showering. I started by meeting the maintenance man and getting a full description of the shower heads he uses and any maintenance records for that specific hotel room. I then asked for access to the specific room with the original head that allegedly shot off and hit the subject. I took my video camera and set it up to record an attempt to duplicate the incident. I screwed on the shower head and turned the water on full force. With my video recording, I turned the shower head a half rotation counterclockwise. I kept doing this until finally the shower head was being held on by just one thread. Water was spraying everywhere, and finally, as the last thread was loosened, the head just dropped straight down into the tub. There was no pressure or force that could have turned the shower head into a dangerous projectile as described by the guest. I also secured a statement from the maintenance man, ruling out any similar accidents having ever been reported. I photographed the threads of the shower waterspout as well as the threads on the shower head itself to show that they were not worn or damaged. I then confiscated the shower head itself as an evidence item. My final report determined that the accident could not have occurred as asserted. When we tried to contact and confront the hotel guest who reported the incident, we found that his name and address were fictitious, and that this was just another common scammer trying to make a quick buck.

Staged fraudulent and exaggerated accidents are so prevalent that an entire service industry of professional claims investigators has arisen. Many investigative agencies' staff case loads are full of these cases. Large corporations, retailers, and insurance carriers are the often victims of these crimes. We explore every imaginable fraud scheme from faked deaths to stolen artwork, to cases of arson.

In a suspected arson, the fire marshal's office may be investigating the incident with a full staff of professional "cause and origin" experts. They may clearly feel that it was arson, but they are under no specific time frame to complete their investigation and produce a report. On the other hand though, the property owner may want to be paid for their loss so that they can rebuild or relocate. They may even need a daily allowance so that they can stay in a hotel while the insurance company processes their claim. The adjuster with the insurance company is on a tight timeline, but he or she cannot control the fire department's investigation. But the professional PI should be able to introduce himself or herself as an agent of the insurance company to get a feel for the direction of the investigation. We call this conducting a "parallel investigation," acquiring information that may not yet be released but staying on top of all developments so that information can be quickly relayed back to our client. If the fire department states that this was arson, then the case may quickly turn to who set the fire and why. These suspicions usually fall first on the car, house, or business owner. This is now an investigation well within the scope and capabilities of any PI. Since the property owner is our insured, they are required to cooperate in any investigation or inquiry we need to conduct to process his or her claim. If he or she doesn't cooperate, the claim for benefits will be denied. We need to know if the owner was behind in his or her payments for the property or if he or she was having financial problems. Was there a problem with the business? Was it failing? Was the car having mechanical difficulties, or was it a part of a hotly contested nasty divorce, or are the owners under water in the evaluation of the property? If the fire was *not* arson and is attributed to some faulty electrical work in a back addition, then the investigation may shift again to a full investigation focusing on the electrical work. This investigation will consist of gathering information to determine who did the electrical work in the addition as this party may be at fault for the loss. The PI will search for the building permits identifying the electrician. If there were no permits pulled and no plans or building inspections made, then the work may have been done illegally and improperly. Insurance companies do not cover illegal acts, and the fire damage may not be covered.

When investigating a homeowner burglary, we usually meet with the homeowner, pick up a copy of the police report, and look for the forced-entry point. We review with the homeowner each stolen item, asking where it was located and what brand it was and ask for any of the accessories that may go with the item, such as a manual or remote control. We may also ask if they have any pictures with the items in the background or being worn by the subject (if it was jewelry). We are not only trying to verify the validity of a claim, but we also are concerned with exaggerations that add costs to the claim. Ironically, I have investigated many homeowner burglaries, and each time a TV set is reported as stolen, it is always described as a "Sony." If a fur coat is taken from the closet, it is always a "Blue Fox." I always ask to see where the coat was hanging in the closet and take a picture. Many times the closets are so full that there isn't even room for a thick, bulky fur. This is when I ask for pictures of the subject wearing the coat. If a video camera is stolen, I ask to see the box, the manual, the remote. The same holds true for a TV. I ask to see pictures of the same room with the TV present. Once again, there may be a financial motive for the owners of the property to have made the claim or loss. Some of the items may have been financed, and the owners may currently be unable to make payments. There may have been a split in the household: two roommates leave and one takes property that the other wanted, or the property was taken by a family member or friends, and the owner feels that reporting it stolen is an easier way to handle the situation.

Whatever type of investigation you may be called to conduct, chances are that someone has worked a similar case before. Outlines of what to do and what to look for are prevalent within our industry.

Forensic computer investigations are also an increasing specialty used by businesses to determine information theft, web-surfing, improper internal e-mail, or other communications not sanctioned or authorized by the company. In domestic cases the client spouse can authorize the PI to forensically examine the computer or even install key tracking software that will capture all correspondence. Statistics show that 22 percent of men and 14 percent of women admitted to having sexual relations outside their marriage sometime in their past. And 17 percent of divorces in the United States are caused by infidelity. Results show that Internet users devote three hours each week to online sexual exploits. Twenty-five percent felt that they lost control of their Internet sexual exploits at least once, or the activity caused problems in their lives. Millions of people visit chat rooms yearly and have multiple "special friends," but only 46 percent of men believe that online affairs are adultery. According to a divorce magazine article, 80 percent think that it's okay to talk with a stranger identified as the opposite sex in a chat room. It is currently estimated that one-third of divorce litigation is caused by online affairs. Because of the anonymity, affordability, and accessibility of Internet sexual resources, the computer can accelerate relationships. This same article reported that 57 percent of people have used the Internet to flirt. Thirty-eight percent of people have engaged in explicit online sexual conversation, and 50 percent of people have made phone contact with someone they chatted with online.

The professional PI can utilize special industry-strength software and hardware to retrieve the truth from any computer. This software can be easily loaded on a thumb drive for an at-home visit by a field investigator. With some research you can find a product that can identify information deleted or hiding on a hard drive. Other software can monitor all computer and Internet activity and take snapshots of the websites visited, e-mails sent and received, instant messages sent and received, chat room conversations, and other computer and Internet activity that is done on a client's PC.

Other domestic investigations involve background checks on couples, renters, business partners, and disputes between neighbors.

Others may choose to support the corporate human resource industry and handle pre-hiring background checks, sexual harassment allegations, workplace violence, or unsafe conditions.

Then there are jobs with criminal and civil defense and plaintiff attorneys, seeking to provide evidence to support their client's position. It is common for the PI to secure statements, find witnesses, and take pictures of an accident location, car, or piece of equipment involved in an accident. If you are interested in working as an investigator in a law firm, you will meet new clients and secure the details of their incident / accident. You will get a copies of police reports and find and secure witness statements.

In criminal cases, you may need to locate a witness or obtain evidence that can support your client's alibi or show that he or she was somewhere different and could not have been involved in the criminal matter.

I found my career specializing in insurance defense work. This area is perhaps the most stable and career-oriented. There are many large agencies that specialize in this industry. It's also an area open to young professionals seeking a rewarding career. Many of these large investigative companies recruit directly out of college, so during a career exhibition, don't shy away from an investigative firm's booth. If the company has an insurance or claims-related title like "Claims Resource or Claims Verification," don't pass up the opportunity to learn what they have to offer. There are many very well run nationwide investigative firms that exclusively serve the insurance industry. Their operations include fully staffed regional offices and field personnel strategically located throughout the United States. These organizations attract and retain the highest caliber of investigative professionals you'll find in any organization. Some have been referred to as the "FBI" of insurance investigations. They employ an exceptionally large and diverse team with a wide variety of educational backgrounds and experience. The field is competitive, and the investigators are true career professionals.

Often, I meet people who, after successful fields in other industries, decide to get into private investigations. They are usually retired or more financially stable and have always wanted to work in the PI industry. I recall a woman who went through a divorce and had difficulty finding a reasonably priced investigator to take on her case. Or a guy whose business was broken into and burned to the ground by a suspected competitor and couldn't get an investigator to take his case. Then there's Zoe, who, at fifty-four, and after being in real estate, decided that she wanted to track down heirs to surplus tax deed sales. The retired, hobby or second career investigators constitute just 1 out of every 5 investigators. Investigators like Zoe, work in small agencies many times solo or with a few like-mind co-workers. The larger agencies employ 100's of investigators and recruit young professionals looking to start and establish a career in the industry.

Many of the most successful agencies have been able to learn to "flat rate" their pricing so that the customer or client has a fixed cost in mind. This, however, is still a lagging practice throughout the industry with many smaller agencies.

For a person wanting to start his or her own agency with little to no experience, he or she may find success specializing in domestic investigations and infidelity. While this has never been my area of concentration, I have done my fair share of domestic cases for friends, business owners, and colleagues. I have always found that giving the client a flat-rate price makes the decision to use your services easier. I suggest packaging surveillance five hours at a time ($250.00–$300.00) and elicit the assistance of the client spouse. Next, creating a "window of opportunity" is the best approach to saving time. Have the spouse you are working for tell the significant other that they need to leave town for work, to comfort a sick family member or help move a friend. Your client-spouse needs to leave in the late afternoon and state they will be back the following day around noon. Whatever the excuse your client uses, the destination needs to be at least three hours away, and the client-spouse needs to call the other spouse right when they leave and again when they get to their destination. I suggest having the client leave at 2:00 p.m.–3:00 p.m., so by 5:00 p.m. he or she is about three hours away. Meanwhile, the PI should arrive on the suspected cheater's place of work, prior to the end of their shift, assuming he or she works from 8:00 a.m.–5:00 p.m. By 4:00 p.m., the client should call the spouse and report his or her location, hopefully several hours from home. Meanwhile, the investigator is on-site with the cheater's car in view at his or her place of employment so that at 5:00 p.m., when work is over, the "window of opportunity" opens. It's just too tempting for the cheater not to use this time period. If the spouse does not see the other party, then the relationship has probably been discontinued. If the client believes otherwise, suggest conducting the same procedure on another weekend.

Also, keep in mind that GPS trackers can also be used to supplement any similar investigation.

WHOSE SIDE ARE YOU ON ANYWAY?

What I am going to say next may go against everything else you have ever heard about investigative work or report writing. It may even go against prior training you have had as a police officer, military investigator, or detective. Investigators who come from a law enforcement environment are routinely told to keep their opinions out of a report and report just the facts. It is typical that a supervisor or attorney will analyze your information and want to be the one who evaluates your results. But not all cases or work you do will be for attorneys, and the insight that a PI can provide may be a thought that hadn't crossed your client's mind. It is important for us to make sure that our position, and the evidence that supports it, is clearly made to our client. Think of it this way: an attorney will take a case, and in a courtroom setting deliver an opening argument based on what he or she wants you to believe. The argument will emphasize his or her side of what happened or what he or she wants you to believe happened. A PI will do the same thing by using the information he or she develops and paint a picture with facts that will emphasize his or her client's best interests. The bottom line is that in order to be valuable to our clients we need to serve their interests. This means that we need to develop information helpful to the reason we were hired. As a professional investigator, you're responsible for conducting a thorough investigation and getting results that will sway an opinion or promote an alternative position supported by your client and the information you developed on his or her behalf.

Whether you like it or not, you are not impartial. You work for your client, and you are looking to develop information helpful to him or her, not information detrimental to them. This is the *business* side of being a private investigator. You need to understand that it's not just reporting the facts, regardless of what they are. It is your job to interpret your findings or to look for new data or evidence that supports your client's interests and report it in a light most favorable for your client. Throughout your report you need to keep in mind your position and strategy. The private investigator hired by OJ Simpson didn't look for evidence that pointed to him being guilty. He was developing information to show or imply his innocence.

I am going to make a simple analogy to further my point. Let's say that my client was reported to have selfishly drank an unfair portion of water from a glass. My investigation determined that the glass was half filled, which, of course, I report as "half full," not wanting to give the impression that it was returned half empty. Also, during my investigation, I learned that the glass was never filled to the top. I secured a statement from a witness that stated, "The glass was never actually filled all the away to the top." I also included another statement from another witness that saw my client drink from the glass and felt that he or she took a smaller sip than anyone else. So now, after my investigation and the collection of statements, I prepare a report that states that according to my witnesses, the glass was never actually filled to the top, and my client drank less than everyone else; therefore, my client did not selfishly drink more than his or her fair share. In every case we must defend or serve an interest of our client. We do not fabricate any evidence; we search out facts that are beneficial to our client or offer an argument opposing any claim made against our client.

Early in my career I worked a rape case on Marco Island. I was not chasing the rapist; he had already been arrested. But his victim was a middle-aged female who lived in a condominium complex and had hired an attorney to sue the complex. The condominium was being renovated, and the construction workers were given temporary passes to get inside the gated complex. One of the workers decided to come in at night, after noticing a female that lived alone in one of the units. The attorney for the victim alleged that there was "a lack of security" in the place since the workers who were not residents had access to the community. He asserted that by giving out temporary passes, it defeated the security system in place and left the residents vulnerable and unsafe. While what happed to the victim is tragic, my job was to defend my client, the condominium association and the insurance carrier providing the liability insurance policy. Commercial buildings, like offices, condominiums, and apartment complexes, carry insurance coverage called liability insurance to protect them from liability issues leading to lawsuits. A common claim by a victim of an act of violence (whether in a business, store, parking lot, or residential building like the condominium case I was working) is that the area is dangerous to those patronizing the establishment or residing in the community, and that the business entity failed to create a safe environment. Before starting a lawsuit, the attorney will file a claim for damages, citing a "lack of security."

In the Marco Island case, I found that the general contractor had conducted background checks on all of his workers, and I took statements and obtained copies of the documents to support this fact. The worker charged with the offense had never been arrested before, and his background check (conducted by a vendor for the contractor) showed a clean record. I double-checked to see if perhaps the background check conducted was flawed and requested a statewide criminal history search through the Florida Department of Law Enforcement (FDLE). They too showed a clean record prior to his arrest for the rape charge. The complex grounds, as a whole, were well-lit, and the residents had always felt secure in the complex and had felt that the lighting was adequate to promote a sense of security.

Marco Island is not what you would consider a high-crime area. On the contrary: it is an upscale community and accommodates upscale residents and visitors. So, why the security gates in this complex? Crime was statistically low is this area, but for the type of clientele they attracted, the security gates seemed more like a status symbol and consistent with the other properties in the upscale communities of Naples and Marco Island. Personally, having penetrated every gated community in which I have been tasked to work in, I think they offer a false sense of security, but nonetheless, in this case, my objective was to gather information that would be helpful in the defense or the allegation regarding the community's lack or breach in security. My next step was to determine just how much crime there was in the area and determine how a reasonable person would interpret that information. I requested a "crime grid" from the local police department. A crime grid is an area, specified by the requester, for all crime in a particular area. The crime can be broken down by categories, such as thefts, burglaries, murders, assaults, etc. While I usually ask for a crime grid for a four-square-block area around my client's property, in this case I just asked for all crimes within the Marco Island zip code since the island is only about a mile in radius. I planned on plotting all of the violent crimes on a large map of the island to see how close they came to my client's complex. What I found even surprised me and ultimately became our main defense. Within the Marco Island zip code, I found that in the past ten years, there had been only three rapes, and two of the rapes had been conducted by the same individual. The third rape was committed on our property by the construction worker with no prior arrest history. So in the past ten years, prior to our event, there had been only one rapist on Marco Island. We also put together information identifying other similar properties in the area—all of which had security gates—to argue that these security gates were expected features of the properties in this market and not in any way associated or related to current crime statistics.

LOCATE INVESTIGATIONS

Many investigations will require the knowledge of how to locate someone. As soon as I am asked to conduct a locate investigation, I immediately review all the information the client provided. Many times the key to finding the subject will be in the information provided. The client may say that he or she checked the subject's former address, and the subject is no longer there. But this address may have been a rental, and the client never thought to identify the landlord or owner of the property and call them for a forwarding address.

Do not hesitate to ask your client for additional information after you have reviewed the information that he or she has provided. Keep your client involved with the investigation and where it's going. You do not want to report something to your client, after several days of hard work, only to discover that a particular fact was already known by them. Unfortunately, your client won't tell you everything in the first interview. Not that they are trying to hide things from you, but what you may consider important clues in your investigation, the client may not. That's why you must make him or her part of what you're doing and keep your client up-to-date. Also, if your client is part of the decision-making process and a given decision costs him or her more time and money, it is easier for the client to accept the extra charges.

Always remember that almost anyone can be found. The steps listed in this lesson are part of the methodology for a locate investigation on a subject who has moved. It is not intended to cover the steps for an abducted person or child.

Pay special attention to this step-by-step locate investigation, and you will find that these are very similar to the steps utilized when conducting a thorough background investigation in relation to your subject. Always keep in mind that investigative work is both scientific and artistic in its application. Learn how to effectively use the resources available to you.

Americans move from place to place more than any other nation of people. Twenty-five percent of us move every year. We move to take advantage of new employment or a business opportunity, to change our lifestyle, to continue our education, or to be closer to our families and friends. To think that every locate assignment you get will be like finding a needle in a haystack would be highly incorrect. Most of the time, we are hired because our clients just don't have the time or know where to begin to look.

Although I know that I may be forgetting a case or two, it's actually really difficult for me to recall not being able to locate a person my client sought. I would imagine that most of my competitors would say the same thing because that's just the nature of our business. Your only limitations are usually time, money, and imagination. The fact is, given unlimited resources, a person's face could be plastered all over the TV one evening, and within hours of the first broadcast, you may find the phone ringing off the hook with where that missing person was two minutes earlier—with precise accuracy. After all, remember: most people we attempt to locate as investigators are former employers, employees, accident witnesses and sometimes our client's client. These subjects *are not* on the list of America's Most Wanted. Also, there is a high probability that the investigator will be able to locate a good address for the subject just by running his or her name in one of our national databases.

Again, you need to keep in mind that we are typically looking for ordinary citizens. They are not missing-persons cases, thank *God*. Just in Florida, there are an estimated nine thousand private investigators, and this would be a very sad world if we worked child-abduction cases every day. Don't get me wrong: nationally, missing and exploited children is a growing problem. However, organizations like The National Center for Missing & Exploited Children have worked hard with law enforcement to dramatically increase the recovery rate for missing children to roughly 90 percent today. Organizations like this have specific procedures in place and work with the missing child's family and local law enforcement.

As a "for-hire" investigator, most of your case work will come from business clients, such as attorney firms, corporations, and insurance companies that are looking for witnesses, defendants, and former employees.

The following are step-by-step procedures the professional investigator uses in a standard locate investigation.

STEP 1: The first step of your locate investigation is to simply run a database search with a reputable database firm offered by companies like Lexis Nexis or TLO. Although you are looking for the most current address on file, don't overlook the oldest address identified either. If the newest address is one that has already been determined to be invalid or is no longer good, move your attention to some of the oldest addresses. Many times you will find that the oldest address is that of a parent or grandparent. In all cases you are looking for telephone numbers (verified and unverified) that you can call to inquire about the whereabouts of the subject. Remember: you want to first do as much work as you can without leaving your office. Make sure you print the comprehensive report and have it with you to cross reference information or as a reference in the field during your investigation.

STEP 2: Utilizing your same database, run just the *address* and leave the search name blank. This will identify all of the people who lived at that address over time. What you are looking for is the name of a subject appearing during the same time period your subject was also reported to be at the same address. This overlapping information may indicate that your subject resided at that location with a roommate, family member, ex-spouse, or friend. Again, always look for any telephone numbers listed for any subject associated to your subject's address and call every number.

STEP 3: Your next step is to cross-reference your subject, as well as anyone else identified as a possible associate, through the sunbiz. org corporate and business database. This will identify any potential businesses your subject or a related person may be involved in. Remember: you are not just looking for corporations but also for fictitious name filings as well. The broadest search tool should be used in each category by searching under officers and registered agents. Once again any business entity should be contacted. Look through the corporate filings or annual reports for telephone numbers listed on the bottom of the pages as contact numbers for the business. Search the Internet for any website under that business name and query the Contact Us page to send e-mail requests.

STEP 4: Google each person's name to identify any other pertinent information that may be available online and follow any lead identified.

STEP 5: Search on-line county property records through the property appraiser's office to determine the owner/landlord of any real property occupied and suspected to be or have been occupied/ rented by your subject to determine the owners name and address for follow-up contact if necessary.

STEP 6: Your next search online will include any available county court records. Here, you are going to check your subject's name for any recorded records civil or criminal. If your subject has a record, his or her file folder will contain additional information. The full file can be reviewed in person by making a personal visit to the courthouse. Criminal records can contain vital information, such as known aliases, employers, and telephone numbers. Court documents will also provide specific information regarding the charges brought against your subject and the circumstances of the initial arrest. Traffic court records will tell you what your subject was driving and list your subject's address at that time. They may even have a scanned copy of the envelope that he or she used to mail in his or her payment with containing a return address.

Civil records identified will show any suits filed against your subject or any suits that your subject may have filed. The civil division will also record any liens against your subject or the subject's property or any liens that your subject may have filed against others. The civil division also contains records of marriage and divorce.

Occupational licenses are also routinely available online or can be searched in-person to identify any business the subject may have in the county or city. Also, check the Uniform Commercial Code (UCC) filings in the civil division. A UCC filing is for loans secured with collateral, such as machinery, equipment, and any asset that may not have a title or registration. Once again, discovering this paperwork may lead you to a better address for the subject that may have otherwise escaped you or possibly even an unknown business he or she operates which was learned through the type of collateralized equipment you found in a UCC filing. Also, check with the probate court in the city where the subject was last known to reside. The probate court will be a source for any wills your subject may have filed or be the executor of and any adoptions or guardianships your subject may be involved in.

STEP 7: By this point, you have already located about 99 percent of the people you have been requested to locate. However, if you still haven't found your subject, you will need to step it up a notch and invoke some help. Without a doubt the social website of Facebook has dramatically changed the landscape of social interaction. We can now not only look for the subject on Facebook, but we can solicit all of his or her friends to have the source contact us. Power in numbers is a great thing, and don't be shy about the numbers part! Ask as many of his or her "friends" to tell the source that you need to speak to them and to call you, or you can even ask if someone has a contact number or e-mail. I was recently hired to find several former employees of a company, who witnessed a slip-and-fall accident. The employees' personnel files had been reviewed, and they were identified as seasonal workers who had at-

facebook

Facebook helps you connect and share with the people in your life.

tended a local university. I found two of the four rather quickly, secured their statements, and then moved on to the other two, searching them on Facebook. One of the subjects was identified as living in Atlanta, but the other subject seemed to have a more checkered address history and still eluded me. He had been evicted from his last two addresses, and the landlords of each had no idea of his current whereabouts or were reluctant to get involved. In one of the evictions I found, it was an out-of-state uncle who actually owned the condominium and evicted his nephew. I elicited the help of about ten of his "friends" on Facebook. Prior to this I had already found his mother, uncle, and grandfather. I spoke to all of the sources, and while I felt that they knew where he lived, they were unwilling to assist me. When I did not get an immediate reply from anyone on Facebook, I put the names of the family members and their addresses in my report and suggested that subpoenas be directed to their attention as they had indicated to me several times that they were in occasional contact with the subject that I needed to locate. I considered this a completed assignment, three and a half out of four, until four months went by, and out of the blue, the subject called me and said, "I heard you were looking for me." The real truth was that I had long closed that file, but wanting to improve my record to 100 percent, I took down his current address and telephone number and sent it to my client!

STEP 8: Sometimes the best address we end up finding is a post office box. In these cases, I usually go to the counter and advise that I am attempting to serve the subject or locate them for pending litigation. I simply show my private investigator's ID and let them do the rest of the assuming. In these cases, the less you say the better. In order to maintain a post office box, a physical address *must* be on file. If the postmaster shows me the address and I already know it is no longer valid, I tell them so. I ask the postmaster if he will lock the mailbox so that when the subject comes to the post office he or she won't be able to access their mail box and will be forced to come to the counter to inquire about their mail. Sometimes they just hold the mail and place a card inside the box saying, "See post office supervisor." Either way the subject is forced to the counter, at which point the postmaster or postmistress can advise the subject that they need to provide an updated address. Prior to leaving, I ask the postmaster or postmistress if I can call the post office in a week's time to get the subject's updated physical address. While this delays your case for a while, it usually works like clockwork and saves you from needing to stake out the post office box, waiting for the subject to come check his or her mail.

I have also found not to ever overlook the value of the local postal carrier who services the route of your subject's last known address. If he or she is in the area during your visit of the last known address, make sure you speak to him or her. The postal carrier sees your subject's mail, and if you think they don't pay attention, you're wrong. Postal carriers know a lot about the people they deliver to; some know more than others, but always talk to them. They often know what type of car your subject drives and possibly where he or she works. When questioning the postal carrier, be polite and sincere and don't forget to say thank you.

STEP 9: If you still haven't found the subject, then you need to get even more aggressive. You need to refocus on what you know about where he or she used to work and live. The subject's past employer and co-workers are all valuable sources of information and may still be in touch with the subject. The subject's previous landlord or apartment manager may provide valuable information as to where he or she is. One of them may have a copy of a lease application filled out by the subject, containing information such as references or a nearest relative's contact information. Any known friends or associates of the subject may have the key to where the subject is hiding. If the subject has an ex-husband or wife, and you can locate him or her, they may be very willing to give you a current address or provide information that will assist you.

STEP 10: Make a personal visit to the physical neighborhood of the subject's last known address. The subject may not have left a forwarding address at the post office for his or her mail, but, most likely, he or she made friends with some people in the area before moving out. These neighbors may have maintained contact with the subject and know where he or she is living at this time. When conducting this type of face-to-face canvas, don't forget the children that you see in the area. Children have a habit of being very honest and forthcoming with information when questioned in the right way. Now, when I say question the children in the neighborhood, keep in mind that you must exercise extreme discretion when attempting to do this. Don't drive down the streets of suburban America in your black sedan, roll down the window, and ask children to come over to your car. Use your head and let common sense prevail.

I was working in Arizona and assigned to locate a subject, and after reviewing the subject's file, I initiated a neighborhood canvas at the subject's last known address. The residents at this address turned out to be the subject's family members: his mother, father, brothers, and sisters. As I approached the residence, there were several young children, approximately nine or ten years old, playing baseball in the front yard. I walked up to the front yard, picked up the baseball, and started playing catch with the kids. After five or ten minutes and a couple of pitches later, I asked one of the children if Johnny, my subject, was home. The child stated to me that his brother Johnny hadn't lived at home for over a year. The child then continued to tell me that his brother Johnny had moved out to Colorado and was a cook at a ski lodge called the Big Bear. Moments later, I proceeded to the residence and knocked on the door. The door was answered by Johnny's mother. Using an appropriate pretext, I asked the subject's mother if Johnny was home or if she knew where I could reach him. She stated to me that she hadn't seen her son for well over a year, and that he was nothing but trouble. For the next five minutes, she continued to tell me what a disappointment her son had been, repeating that she had no contact with him and had no idea where he was. Keep in mind that when you question sources close to your subject, such as relatives or friends, they may try to cover up the truth. As I got back to my office, I looked up the Big Bear and found a Colorado resort by that name on the Internet. I obtained a telephone number for the resort, called up, and asked for the restaurant. I spoke with a hostess at the restaurant and asked for Johnny. The hostess told me that she didn't think he was in yet but to hold on, and she would check the schedule. She returned moments later and informed me that Johnny was scheduled to begin work that afternoon at 4:00 p.m. She told me that Johnny was a cook and worked Tuesday through Sunday from 4:00 p.m. until closing.

Following a specific plan of action, I made a personal visit to Johnny's last known address to conduct a thorough canvass of the area. I found this residence to be Johnny's parents' house. Here I discreetly questioned Johnny's little brother, who gave me the information I felt was valid. Had I not gotten the information from Johnny's brother, I would have been much more aggressive with his parents. Parents, despite their differences, usually know how to reach their children.

STEP 11: You may have a list of court case files you identified from your on-line records searching and want to investigate the matters further. The entire file, many times still paper, can only be reviewed by making a personal visit to the county courthouse. Each county courthouse is different, and while most are online, the record you see online will only be a brief fraction of the information you can get by pulling and reviewing the actual paper file. If you are in a small county, be extremely polite and courteous; you will get more assistance with a pleasant attitude. You should also be thinking about developing a friend on the inside that you can call to obtain information instead of making the drive. The best investigators are always thinking about developing their sources.

STEP 12: Hopefully, by following this step-by-step location guide, you have found your subject by now. Remember that the subject's social security number can establish which state your subject applied for his or her social security account in. It is usually your subject's home state, a state your subject may return to, especially in times of trouble. Your subject may have friends or relatives to stay with or be near or from which to receive assistance. Somewhere during your investigation, a city or town in that state may have been uncovered or mentioned in passing that will help lead you to your subject.

STEP 13: A motor vehicle registration or MVR search can usually be obtained at the county tax office. These records are also part of the typical database search run through Lexis Nexis or TLO. This information is generally available to the public, although it is considered protected information by a handful of states. Any license plate numbers associated to your subject should be run to identify the owner. You may have a tag of a car your subject was seen driving in or obtained a ticket in for speeding. The tag can be cross-referenced to identify the owner's name, date of birth, and address.

STEP 14: State driver's license, or DL, information is also commonly accessed by the professional investigator. Driver's license information can be obtained in virtually every state, with a few exceptions. Certain states restrict access by requiring that you have your subject's driver's license number before they will give you any information. This number can be obtained from the database report run in STEP 1. With the driver's license information, you can determine whether or not your subject has a valid license. It may also show tickets from another state, indicating that he or she has moved. Many county courthouses throughout the state sell seven- and twelve-year DL records. Call ahead and make certain that you are not wasting a trip to the courthouse. These records are also available online through your database source or another online specialty search company for a fee.

STEP 15: The local or city utility department is another possible source for locating your subject. Many times these utility services are public utilities and, as such, their records are available for review to the public. If the information from the local utility department is not readily accessible to the general public, then consider developing an inside source whenever possible.

STEP 16: If you've followed all these steps and are still unable to locate your subject, don't overlook the Department of Corrections, the DOC. Your subject may be receiving three square meals a day, safe and sound in a state correctional facility. With your subject's name and social security number, you can query the supervised population database of the Department of Corrections (DOC) in virtually every state across the country and determine whether your subject is incarcerated at this time. The same holds true for the federal prison system.

STEP 17: If you still have not found the subject of your investigation, double-check your database to see if you see DOD after his or her name, indicating the date of death. This information is obtained from the SSN death benefits database, which is part of most national comprehensive databases.

TOOLS OF THE TRADE

There is no better source or tool than an informant or someone who lives in the area and knows or works with the subject being investigated and who wants to tell everything they know about him or her. This can save days of field work or guessing. So the investigator's ability to extract information from a subject, whether they are a willing participant or an unsuspecting party, is an important skill. Be a good listener to pick up on leads that may need to be explored further to dig deeper into what he or she may know. Be prepared to keep this person talking and ask questions until they appear to no longer have anything to offer. Remember that what you consider important is not always obvious to the interviewee.

I can't tell you how many times I have interviewed neighbors that immediately tell me they know nothing. It is only after finding a way to get them talking and keep them talking that I learn that they do have helpful information. Don't leave the area until you have spoken to every neighbor within eyesight of the subject's house. Leave notes on the doors of those that are not home at the time of your neighborhood visit, but be evasive about your interest. Just write down on the paper that you're an investigator looking into a matter and need to speak to them. Leave your cell phone number so that they can reach you directly. If they don't call, plan on making a return visit in the evening or on a weekend when you may have a greater chance of finding them home.

No matter how many people tell you that they don't know anything about your subject, forge on and always remember to ask about any children and where they might attend school. Do they know where the subject or his wife used to work? Many times you just need to keep them talking, and suddenly they respond, "Oh, yeah, his wife works at my daughter's middle school." I recall one neighbor who stated over and over again that he had no idea where my subject moved and seemed to be of no help, only to turn back to me as if a light bulb turned on in his head and said that my subject's wife worked at the convenience store down the street.

People are busy, and sometimes our inquiries are seen as interruptions of their valuable time regarding a matter that doesn't involve them. It's a necessary step that needs to be approached with sensitivity and respect. The way you make this contact will largely determine the amount of information you will get in response.

It's also not unusual to go from one town to the next, following leads in a locate investigation. People will be crucial to speak with, and we need to cover a lot of ground quickly. I recall trying to do field work without my "Garmin" GPS on my dash giving me voice command directions as a reminder to stay on course. In fact, for years, I argued with my wife that I did not need a GPS because I had MapQuest on my phone, and before that I printed out directions to my surveillance or investigation prior to leaving the house. I just couldn't justify why I should pay money for another device that I really didn't think I needed. But I couldn't have been more incorrect, and after almost three years of refusing the device, I received one from Santa. I didn't realize how much time I had wasted following a map, looking up driving directions, or just getting lost because I wasn't paying attention. And in those cases where I would go to one address and find my subject no longer lived there and then needed to follow-up and visit several other addresses, the GPS was incredible in getting me from one location to the next in the shortest amount of time. And even in surveillances when I was following someone on a day of errands and then entering their address as we headed back, I saw that I could foresee all of the subject's turns. Then there were those cases when I thought the subject was purposely taking me into a quiet residential area or attempting to detect a tail, but my GPS reassured me that this was a shortcut back to the subject's house. Other times, I would be working a case interviewing one person in one place then learning of another witness in another area, only to learn of two more witnesses somewhere else, and when calling them I could enter their addresses in my GPS and let the witnesses know my estimated time of arrival to secure their statements.

While one GPS helps us find an address, another GPS can be used to track our subjects. The magnetic detachable covert GPS tracker is very hot on the PI tool list.

In 2011, a New Jersey woman hired a PI who used a GPS tracker to track her cheating husband. Her husband sued his wife for invasion of privacy, but the judge wrote that tracking him was in the public domain and therefore felt that it was not an invasion of his privacy. Many times, when GPS tracking is used, it is treated like other sensitive tactics and never mentioned in the investigative report or disclosed to a client. In the New Jersey case, the PI felt more comfortable by giving the tracker to his client and having her place the device on the cheater's vehicle. Having the spouse place the device on the car seems to be a tactic used by PIs to distance themselves from the act itself. Many PI agencies offer the leasing of these devices to their clients. Since this is a relatively new field device, there are very few court cases on which its use has been ruled. Case law in this area will be closely watched until definitive laws are passed addressing the legal use of the GPS tracker.

There are two types of GPS trackers: real-time "data pushers" and "data loggers." Real-time data pushers enable the real-time tracking and following of a person's travels by information being transmitted from the tracker to a computer, tablet or smartphone while the subject is moving. These types of units require broadband service or cellular contract. The second type of tracker, known as a data logger, keeps information stored within the unit, and after the unit is retrieved, the information is downloaded to a computer and cross-referenced with a map or software like Google Maps to show the exact route and locations that the subject traveled while being tracked. Data loggers are less expensive and can be used as an investigative tool to identify routes and places of interest visited by the target.

For "live" surveillance, real-time trackers are preferred but may not be permitted or an acceptable practice, depending on your client. It's important to know the law, and currently in Florida there is no statute making this a criminal matter. However, a civil complaint and lawsuit could be filed, and as a PI, the last thing we want is to be personally brought into a lawsuit as a result of a case we are working. These units, however, have become so stealth and beneficial that their use in the industry will only continue to grow.

TAKING STATEMENTS

I t's very common to conduct interviews and secure written or re-corded statements along the way as supporting evidence in a case. Statements are taken to document a witness's knowledge or facts about a matter and to memorialize this information while it's still fresh in his or her mind. Within the statement we will want to get as much personal information about the witnesses as possible, keeping in mind that this case may go on for a year, two, or several, for that matter. So getting what we call identifying information about the witness as well as other family members will make locating them a lot easier when the time comes to produce them as witnesses. We know 25 percent of the nation's population moves every year, so the more information you can get without being too overbearing will prove well worth it if your witness is one of those that moved.

Interviewing is an art that you will get better at over time. Confidence in your ability to understand what the witness is tell-ing you is critical. If the witness is describing a complicated matter, have them draw it out, show you pictures, or even take you there. Don't move on with your questioning until you understand every detail of what has already been said. Listen carefully as follow-up questions will need to be asked to clarify any uncertainty and are critical to getting those details that can be investigated afterward to corroborate or pierce the truthfulness of the witness's statement. You can never get too many details, and through these details we obtain additional leads to pursue and information to verify. I always act as if I believe his or her story to encourage more details. I will ask more questions that would seem to support their story and possibly needed to verify their statement. Some of the most believable liars are criminals and drug addicts. Both are so used to covering up their tracks that lies come naturally, and they can be incredibly convincing. I just keep them talking so that I have as many details as possible. You may have heard the saying "loose lips sink ships." Well, that's exactly the principle behind getting as much information as possible. My next step will be to use their own story and attempt to verify the details.

Recently I investigated an auto theft, and the owner advised me that her home had also been broken into. Apparently the thief broke into the house and stole the car keys. The owner of the car was hospitalized at the time and was relying on details reported to her by her son. The car had subsequently been involved in an accident near an office park, and after the crash the car thief fled the area on foot. Footage of the thief was caught on an area business's security camera. The person in the video looked very similar to the car owner's son. The image was grainy and distant, but the tall, slender, short-dark-haired twenty-year-old subject seemed to fit him perfectly. He also had a somewhat unique gait, which seemed to be noted in the footage.

Prior to interviewing the son, I learned that he had a history of drug abuse, with his drug of preference, the very addictive prescription pain-killer known as oxycontin. When I met the tall slender male, he was wearing penny loafers, designer jeans, and a sports coat. He began the introduction with a long story about his history and how my difficulty in contacting him was due to working with his father in Daytona Beach and going to school at night. During the interview he reported that he had been at the hospital with his mother for three days over the time period the house was burglarized. He had gone back and forth with a friend twice to get things for his mother, but at the time of the car theft and accident, he was at the hospital. As I let him speak for almost two hours, he provided such incredible details. He advised that on the date of the accident, at 3:00 a.m., which was actually five hours before the accident, he was returning to the hospital from one of those trips home to get some clothes and personal items for his hospitalized mother. He reported that he was driven to downtown Orlando by his friend Josh. At around 3:00 a.m., they stopped at a 7-Eleven on Orange Avenue near the Orlando Regional Medical Center (ORMC) to purchase some items before actually arriving at the hospital. Later that same morning, he stated that he walked to that same 7-Eleven around 8:00 a.m. He stated that the same clerk who waited on him at 3:00 a.m. waited on him again at 8:00 a.m. He described the worker as a dark-skinned "Indian" female in her twenties. He stated that he was certain that she would remember him because he was dressed in "Stewie" pajamas (from *Family Guy*), wearing a black jacket and high leather boots. He also stated that during his first visit there the young woman stopped him from leaving when he forgot to pick up the cigarettes he purchased. During the second visit, she asked if he was still having a rough day. He also stated that when he returned to the hospital, they had just served his mom pancakes, and the hospital serves breakfast at 8:00 a.m. His mother, who was listening in, agreed with everything he was saying. Based on the subject's statement, he could not have crashed the car in Sanford at 8:00 a.m. and also have been in South Orlando at 8:00 a.m.

I determined that there are two 7-Eleven stores within walking distance of ORMC: one located at 1823 South Orange Avenue (referred to as the Kaley Store) and one located at 902 Gore Street. I determined that neither store had a female in her twenties working a third shift. Furthermore, the third-shift girl would not have still been at the store by 8:00 a.m. The witness also stated that the clerk was a darker-skinned Indian or Latin girl, and neither store had any personnel that fit that description working the overnight shift. The managers in both stores agreed to review the video footage for that day, and a follow-up call advised me that the subject was not observed in their stores over the time period stated.

Later that evening I tried to call the subject to clarify if I had the right area or the right stores. I persisted with several more calls to the witnesses, advising that what he had told me did not check out. He never responded.

Always go out and check the information provided in any statement. Talk to all of the people mentioned in the statement or visit any place they said they visited to see if it can be verified. You will find that through thoroughness, you will become a successful investigator. There will be those that stop short of verifying all information or feel that the drive to visit a location is not worthwhile. It's through these little acts of disregard or apathy that a good investigator is separated from a bad one. As investigators, a large part of our work is investigating incidents or accidents. Incidents that occur at work to employees are investigated by the employers' agents and companies that insure employers and their employees. Employers are expected to maintain safe environments for their workers. When a worker is required to clean the windows from the outside of a high-rise building, there are security procedures the worker follows to protect him or her from any workplace dangers. For instance, the worker is required to wear tethers or a body harnesses in case of a fall. Most of us can relate to having auto insurance to cover an automobile accident. Our auto coverage provides protection in case we are injured in the accident or in case we injure someone else. The coverage also reimburses us for the damage to our cars or the cars we struck in the accident. It also covers any other property we may have damaged if, perhaps, for example, we ran into a fence or building that needs to be repaired. In my earlier statements, I mentioned that law enforcement agencies handle criminal matters; however, when these incidents occur many times, a private party is brought into the matter. For instance, if a person is shot at work by an assailant during a robbery, the police will investigate the matter but so will the insurance company that insures the business and its employees. Since this shooting or incident occurred at work and the employee's injuries would be covered by his or her workplace insurance, the insurance company's representative would look into the matter for clarification of what happened. The worker, at the same time, may have been seriously injured and may seek legal representation to assure that his or her best interests are protected. He or she may not be able to go back to work and may have a permanent personal injury or permanent disability. An investigator may be hired by the injured person's attorney to secure all of the facts of the incident. Businesses and property owners are lawfully required to provide guests with adequate security. A lack of proper security that leads to an injury or assault can lead to a premises liability lawsuit.

Very simply, all property owners must maintain a reasonably safe environment for visitors – and this includes keeping those on their premises protected from harm from outsiders. If you were physically harmed or sexually assaulted while on property owned by someone else, they could be liable for your injuries due to lack of security, inadequate security, improper security, or negligent security.

So in any incident or accident, there may be law enforcement investigators working a case and private investigators representing different parties or sides of the matter. The investigators have different responsibilities and objectives. The law enforcement officer is looking to apprehend the assailant. The private investigator hired by the employer or their insurance company is going to look into the workplace environment and the security provided to protect the worker from harm. The PI working in defense of the suit will start to show that the workplace did have the security required to protect the worker based on information collected during the investigation. Issues concerning crime in the immediate area as well as specific incidents of a similar nature occurring at the employer's specific location will all be collected.

The topic of investigating incidents and accidents covers a very broad spectrum. Many incidents and accidents occur while we are at work. Businesses need to know and understand the risks faced by their employees and visitors. The best way to eliminate these risks or liability issues is to investigate the critical components of who, what, where, when, why, and how.

A good statement taker will need to pull details from the witness's memory. There will be details that he or she doesn't realize are important. Before going out, make sure you have a clear understanding of your objective. You can't conduct a thorough interview if all you ask is what happened. Knowing and understanding the reason for the statement is key to even knowing what questions to ask. A client may ask for a statement simply to document his or her file. However, his or her purpose may be to determine liability or subrogation possibilities or to inquire about a possible pre-existing medical condition. You may be verifying an alibi or a previously told story by a corroborating party. There can be many reasons why you are securing the statement, and in order to do well in each instance, you need to prepare. Always have a guide to follow as well as additional specific questions that may be relative to the issue and need to be answered. Always have a note pad to jot down questions that come to you while the witness is talking. Here are the principle points to follow:

REPARATION
Review your assignment and locate a good "base" outline appropriate to the type of statement you are taking. Have a note pad and a diagram sheet available that shows the area in case you need to discuss specific areas. Make your own list of questions as well.
All Statements will follow the basic format, with an INTRODUCTION, BODY OF STATEMENT (questions), and a CLOSING.

PLAN AND CONTROL
Carefully plan the conversation and briefly outline your approach. Take notes during the conversation. Listen to the interviewee's responses. His or her responses should prompt additional clarification questions. Remember, anyone listening to or reading the transcription from a recorded statement should have enough information to understand the information relayed and not have any unanswered questions.

INFORMALITY

Remember to use an informal, positive approach. If you want a person to be your friend, treat him or her as your friend; if you want a recorded statement, treat him or her as if they *will* give you one.

REVIEW

Review the assignment and have all known facts well fixed in your mind.

COURTESY

Remember—courtesy is essential.

RECORDED STATEMENT FORMAT

(Turn recorder on.)

Today's date is (date). My name is (your name). I am employed with (company name), and I am representing (name of client company). I am at (the location where you are taking statement).

I am interviewing (name of subject), who was (involved in the incident / accident, witnessed, etc.).

(Name of person), are you aware that I am recording our conversation? (Response) Do I have your permission to do so? (Response)

BODY OF STATEMENT

Depending on the type of statement, refer to statement outlines and your own prepared notes and questions. Address the specific concerns of the client, such as any special questions indicated on the assignment sheet that must be covered. Be certain that you fully cover and understand how the incident or accident occurred. This should be a relaxed conversation, so put your interviewee and yourself at ease. Don't be afraid to ask questions out of order. If a question comes to mind, ask it. You can rarely ask too many questions.

CLOSING

Ask:

Is there anything else you would like to add or clarify in this statement before I conclude the recording? (Response) (If the response is no, proceed with closing; if the response is yes, let the subject explain and ask follow-up questions, if necessary. Once you are through, repeat this statement again before proceeding.) (Subject's name), were you aware that I was recording our conversation? (Response) Did I have your permission to do so? (Response) (Subject's name), was everything you told me true and correct to the best of your knowledge and belief? (Response) Would you please state your name for the final time? (Response) My name is (Your name). Thank you for voluntarily giving this statement. (Turn recorder off.)

NOTE

When taking a statement, avoid turning the recorder off once the statement is started. If you do, you must say why the recorder is being turned off. When you turn it back on, you need to state that you are continuing with the recording and identify the person and yourself again.

WRITTEN STATEMENT FORMAT

The most obvious difference between the two will be the means in which the statement is taken. Be ready to write for an extended length of time, so find a comfortable writing position at a desk or table.

Make certain that you are using carbonless, *three-part lined statement paper*. This paper is available in stationery stores or on the Internet. The top, original, white copy will be sent to the client with your report. The next (yellow) copy will be stapled to your notes, and the third part should be handed to the person whom the statement was taken from. If you don't have this specialized statement paper, you can still use a note pad with a sheet of carbon paper between the pages. Just one sheet of carbon paper will be fine as a copy can be given to the witness, and the original can be copied for the file back at the office.

The written statement should be taken *as if the person wrote it himself or herself.* **You should, however, write the statement** so that all vital questions are answered. Also, by the investigator writing the statement, the handwriting should be legible or at least understandable by the investigator. The written statement should be a continuous narrative, without any paragraphs or blank spaces. If you make a mistake just cross out the word and write in the correct word, then both parties should initial the correction. Below is an example of how the statement should be written.

Example:

My name is Veronica M. Brown, and I am here today, Monday, February 3, 2014, with James Corn of JB Investigations. We are here today in regard to the (<u>automobile accident, slip-and-fall, stolen property, etc.</u>), which occurred on (<u>date</u>) in/at (<u>location</u>). I am a twenty-five-year-old white female, born on July 7, 1965. I currently reside at 1276 Deer Lake Circle, Apopka, Florida 32712. My telephone number is 904-896-4629. I am married to Tim Brown, who presently works for All-American Gym as the manager (additional witness identification information). On the afternoon of (<u>date</u>) at approximately 2:30 p.m., I was driving home from having just picked my husband up from work. I was driving our 1993 blue Plymouth Voyager with my husband seated on the passenger's side when he yelled to look out! Just then I slammed on my brakes and skidded approximately twenty feet. We were both wearing our seat belts, and I was only driving at approximately forty-five mph, so we stopped in time. The road was dry, and it was a clear day. Since my husband was on the passenger side and staring out the passenger-side window, he noticed a stampeding bull headed right for the road in front of us. We were driving on Old Winter Garden Road, heading south, and my husband was looking toward the east. The guy behind us had been tailgating me for about five miles, ever since I left the gym. At about five miles on Old Winter Garden Road, the area gets real rural, and I guess he felt it was a good place to pass. The guy who was passing me must have been looking for any oncoming cars because he sure didn't see that bull....

Remember, as this hypothetical example exhibits, each line should be continuous, without any large spaces. This will prevent any room to alter or add information to the final statement that was not intended to be part of the statement. Whenever any corrections or error is made, be sure to have the interviewee initial the corrections. Number each page by using "Page 1 of 3; Page 2 of 3; Page 3 of 3," etc.

CLOSING
Have the interviewee initial each page.
Ask the subject whether there is anything else he or she would like to say with regard to this incident. Write exactly what he or she says. If he or she has nothing else to say, close with the following final statement and the interviewee's signature.

"I have read the above statement of _____ pages, and it is true and correct to the best of my knowledge and belief." X (Signature of interviewee)

Detach the last (pink) copy of the three-part statement paper (or the second sheet/ carbon copy) and provide the interviewee with a complete copy of his or her written statement.

PRINCIPLES OF INTERVIEWING

INTERVIEWING	is a specialized way of asking questions.
INTERVIEWING	is the art of extracting the maximum amount of truthful information from an individual.
INTERVIEWING	is the questioning of a person who is believed to possess knowledge that is of pertinent interest to the investigator.

An <u>INTERVIEW</u> is conducted for the purpose of gaining information that may establish the facts of an accident or incident, and that may provide the investigator with leads that will further substantiate the validity of the details.

In an <u>INTERVIEW</u> (claimants, witnesses, subjects, defendants, employers, supervisors, coworkers, etc.), the interviewee usually gives his or her account of the accident/incident in his or her own words and in his or her own way.

In an <u>INTERVIEW</u>, a specialized way and/or technique is used to ask questions.

WITNESS — one who has <u>seen</u> or who <u>knows</u> something concerning the incident under investigation and is competent of discussing it.

SIX BASIC QUESTIONS – must be exploited to the maximum in every interview.

WHO?
WHAT?
WHEN?
WHERE?
WHY?
HOW?

INTERVIEWING DO'S

1. DO provide a suitable place for the interview.
2. DO fix the time for the interview, if possible.
3. DO have the witness conform to your arrangements, if possible.

4. DO show some consideration for the witness, once he or she indicates that they are willing to cooperate.
5. DO seat the witness and place him or her at ease.
6. DO seat the witness so that the light, if any, falls on him or her, if possible.
7. DO show courtesy and politeness toward the ordinary witness.
8. DO create a motive for the witness to provide you with information.
9. DO assure the witness of protection of unnecessary disclosure.
10. DO distinguish between a witness and a bias witness.
11. DO seek to identify the witness's interest with yours, in the mind of the witness.
12. DO seek to win the confidence of the witness.
13. DO obtain basic personal details from the witness.
14. DO make an investigation of the witness before interviewing, if possible.
15. DO find out where the witness may be reached, before the interview is over.
16. DO impress the witness with the importance of what he or she has told you.
17. DO ascertain the sources of the witness's testimony.
18. DO attempt to determine the truthfulness of the witness's testimony.
19. DO let the witness tell his or her story in his or her own words.
20. DO make an estimate of the consistency of the witness's story.
21. DO get the witness's story before he or she can consult others.
22. DO attempt to ascertain the basis of the witness's recollection of important details.
23. DO question continuously—most people talk.
24. DO interview witnesses when they are "hot" or the information is fresh to them.
25. DO observe the behavior of the witness, his or her reaction to questions, hesitancy, and other qualities that characterize his or her responses.
26. DO note all contradictions.

27. DO obtain documentary evidence, when possible, the originals or copies/photographs thereof, using a camera or your phone if necessary.
28. DO change interviewers, if you find that you are "stymied" with a particular witness.
29. DO remember that there are no hard-and-fast rules.
30. DO keep all promises made to a witness.
31. DO look the witness straight in the eye.

INTERVIEWING DON'TS
1. DON'T be rude or impolite. There is matter in manner.
2. DON'T antagonize the witness.
3. DON'T deny or dismiss reasonable requests of the witness once he or she has indicated that they will cooperate.
4. DON'T interview more than one witness at a time.
5. DON'T lose control over the conduct of the interview.
6. DON'T "wisecrack" during an interview.
7. DON'T cross-examine or "grill" the witness.
8. DON'T let the witness know the purpose of the interview.
9. DON'T let suspicion fall on a witness whom you think is suspect, during an interview.
10. DON'T allow the interview to be interrupted, if you can possibly avoid it.
11. DON'T use only the question-and-answer type of interview; look for second- and third-tier follow-up questions.
12. DON'T lose track of, or dismiss, the witness until you have obtained from him or her all the information that he or she has.
13. DON'T ask more than one question at a time.
14. DON'T persist in following an unsuccessful approach.
15. DON'T place much credence in hearsay.
16. DON'T tell the witness what the "story" is; let him or her do the talking.
17. DON'T necessarily disbelieve an entire statement just because part of it is untrue or inaccurate.

18. DON'T ignore valid documentary evidence in favor of oral testimony.
19. DON'T assume that the witness is familiar with the area or any subject matter.
20. DON'T fail to evaluate information accurately.
21. DON'T fail to obtain corroboration of testimony, if possible.
22. DON'T let the witness know how much you know.
23. DON'T lose your temper.
24. DON'T use profane language.
25. DON'T ignore your senses or common sense.
26. DON'T overlook any leads given by the witness.
27. DON'T overlook any slips made by the witness.
28. DON'T argue with the witness.
29. DON'T indulge in personalities.
30. DON'T allow the information that you get to go stale.
31. DON'T allow your prejudices against the witness otherwise influence your evaluation of the witness's testimony.
32. DON'T forget to note the witness's behavior and movements— i.e., any hesitation in answering questions; uneasiness; inability to maintain eye contact.
33. DON'T forget that there are no hard-and-fast rules to interviewing.
34. DON'T lie to the witness or make threats.
35. DON'T forget to indicate the witness's ability in your opinion to recount the incident if necessary in front of a judge and jury.

GETTING STARTED
1. Call the interviewee, introduce yourself, and explain the purpose for your call.
2. Be prepared to fully identify yourself and have a business card available.
3. Dress appropriately.
4. Make certain the batteries in your recorder are fresh and keep spares handy.

5. The first thing to do upon meeting the interviewee is to put him or her at ease. Don't make a big thing of your recording equipment; treat it as a natural part of the procedure. Answer any questions asked, but don't volunteer unnecessary detail about what will or might be done with the recording. If pressed, you can truthfully minimize the likelihood of its use in court, but make no guarantees.

6. Explain what you are going to do is to ask a few questions beforehand, and then you will turn the machine on and go over the same facts.

7. Pre-interview the witness. Ask the questions you intend to ask for the record. This tends to relax the witness and also prepares you for areas of the story that you may want to go into more deeply. Before recording the statement ask the interviewee to have a pencil handy. Invite him or her to make a diagram of the accident as a guide of his or her description. This will help prevent the interviewee from contradiction.

8. It will be a good idea to tell the interviewee that some repetition will be necessary for the purpose of identification and clarification.

9. Place the recording device <u>close to the interviewee</u>. He or she most likely will be the soft-spoken one. You can always purposely speak louder.

10. Use a digital recorder, not any recording application on your phone or other device.

11. Should an interruption occur by another party or yourself, you should keep the recorder playing and comment to explain the interruption, and that the recording will be continued in a few minutes.

12. If the recorder is turned off, you must ask your subject if he or she would like to discuss anything that was mentioned while the recorder was off. A few reasons for turning the machine off would be for the interviewee to answer the phone or door or clear up a complicated matter.

13. Keep each interview separate. Each interview should be a separate mp3 or wav file. These recordings will need to be transferred to your computer case file and also copied for the client as well as a backup copy on disk or external hard drive as evidence inventory.

WHILE RECORDING
1. Begin the recording by following the opening statement in a statement guide you should have pertaining to your particular interview. Be sure to include the question: "Do I have your permission to record this interview?" You must also establish that the witness understands that the conversation is being recorded, and that you have his or her permission to do so.
2. At the beginning of the statement, you should identify people, places, time, and what is being done.
3. You should also establish the fact that he or she is giving you the statement voluntarily, without the promise of any reward and under no circumstances that would constitute a threat or duress of any kind. You need to establish the subject's educational level and his or her ability to read, write, and understand the English language. You also need to understand and establish your subject's control of his or her faculties by asking if he or she is under the influence of any drug, alcohol, or medication of any kind at the time of the recording. If he or she is under a doctor's care and taking some type of drug, you may want to establish what that drug is and at what time it was last taken by your subject. If, at any point and time during this statement, while your subject is providing you with specific information about circumstances that are important to your case, and you have any suspicion that the subject is taking some sort of medication, uses drugs, or is a drinker, you might want to again ask him or her if at the time he or she observed, heard, or was involved in these circumstances, was he or she under the influence of any drugs, alcohol, or medication.

4. If you are taking statements from more than one person at the same location, separate them. Do not allow one to hear the other person's statement.

5. Use good statement-taking techniques during the body of the recording. Control the conversation with the aid of your statement outline. Keep the information factual and use open-ended questions, beginning with <u>who</u>, <u>what</u>, <u>when</u>, <u>where</u>, <u>how</u>, etc.

6. It is also important that you take notes during this recorded statement. You should also have other notes written down prior to actually taking the statement because the outline you may have cannot be comprehensive to all situations. You will also be taking notes while the witness is talking. These follow-up notes constitute what we call second- and third-tier questions. These follow-up questions will be used to bring certain points out during the subject's statement.

7. End the recording, as suggested in the statement guide, by asking if there is anything you haven't covered or any pertinent facts that are felt to be important. If so, let them come out freely. Then ask the witness if he or she understood all of your questions and if his or her answers are true and correct to the best of his or her knowledge. Make sure that the interviewee repeats his or her approval of having the statement recorded. A final "thank you" ends the recording.

AFTER RECORDING

1. After the recording and before you leave, run a spot-check on the record to make sure the machine was working.

2. As soon as possible, while the interview is still fresh, <u>summarize the important facts</u> and <u>your impression of the witness</u>. Indicate how the information developed in the statement may affect the case. This information should be reported on in your report and comprise a vital part of the report conclusion.

3. In most cases your report will substitute for transcriptions of the recording, so don't be afraid to elaborate in detail. Keep in

mind that only at the request of the client will the record be transcribed.

4. Your report and the digital recording then become a "material" part of the file.

5. Remember: as investigators we are not negotiating a settlement with the subject, just getting the facts.

There are many statement outlines available for just about any interview scenario you can think of. Just keep in mind that these outlines should not be considered to be complete and comprehensive. Each case will warrant unique questions that apply to that case alone. They are merely outlines to reference and stimulate your own question-making process and most importantly, listen carefully to the subject so that you can ask follow-up questions

For a statement outline guide consider purchasing my reference book "Claims Investigation Statement Manual by John Bilyk ISBN-10: 0692203176 / ISBN-13: 978-0692203170

It is always advised to take a statement in person so that you can see the subject, study their body language, and generally be more effective. However, there will be cases where a statement may have to be taken over the phone. There are countless devices for taking statements over the phone from a landline. Most of these devices plug into the hand receiver and then have a separate mini-jack that plugs into the recorder. When it comes to taking statements on your mobile phone, you will require an app that allows you to download a program that will record both sides of the conversation. Your phone, however, may not be the best device and may have limitations of time or recording, so it's best to use a device that is specifically designed for this type of function. Sony makes a microphone that plugs

into your digital recorder on one end and an earpiece on the other. The earpiece's primary purpose is to capture the phone conversation you hear as you place your cellular phone over the ear with the microphone earpiece. The device was released in 2012 and is called the **Sony ECM-TL3 Earphone-Style Mini Electret Condenser Microphone.** I purchase my microphone earpiece online through the Sony store for $19.99. Of course, in Florida, you still need to notify the participants before recording any phone conversations. Even if the interview is not a formal statement, you must tell the other party that the call is being recorded. Recording conversations eliminates the challenge of having to write down all the information. It also prevents you from forgetting relevant or important information. I use my Sony ear piece while I am on the phone and driving at the same time when note taking is just not an option.

When choosing a digital recorder, I prefer those with a built-in USB that allows me to just plug it into my computer and transfer and save the file. Many recorders come with a separate USB wire that can add to the amount of stuff you need to carry or misplace. These recorders can be found at large discount stores like Wal-Mart or Kmart from around twenty-five to thirty-five dollars. I am not a big believer in buying expensive equipment when there are so many devices that are reasonably priced and just as dependable. For many years now I have used the RCA VR5220-A Digital Recorder, which takes two AAA batteries and has never let me down. Newer digital recorders will record files in MP3, which are smaller and easier to e-mail. The newer recorders have climbed in pricing to over fifty dollars, but they are well worth the extra money if emailing statements will be a common practice. The MAIN KEY to buying any recorder is to make certain that it has the capability to upload to your computer. Some of the cheaper brands don't have a USB jack for uploading, which are of no value to the investigator, so be careful.

DEVELOPING A PROSPERING BUSINESS CULTURE

When I became a manager in the investigations business, I had a boss that encouraged me to resolve issues at my local office level. If a client called and was unhappy, I knew I had the authority to resolve the issue to the customer's satisfaction. Whether that meant spending more time on a case or crediting a bill, the job of mine was to resolve the issue to the client's satisfaction. I never had to call anyone or ask the person to wait until I discussed the situation with my manager. I realized very early that empowering employees in such a fashion helped build solid relationships with clients. Clients knew that whatever issue or problem arose, I was there to help. This ability to make decisions not only made me feel appreciated but I was respected by my clients. In turn, I felt valuable and used these same concepts in managing those around me. While I knew that any one investigator could be replaced, I preferred to recognize that a good team made me look better, and good people are always worth trying to keep. It's a give-and-take managerial style that warrants both praise and corrective criticism. We routinely held monthly meetings and recognized an investigator each month for his or her performance in the field and created competitiveness between the investigators. We also spoke openly about ways to improve efficiency in the office and the field. In the early 1980s, I remember reading a business article about efficiency and looking for redundancy in the office or your workplace. This was before the

Internet and powerful computers arrived, but we decided to put a printer on each manager's desk so he or she wasn't getting up to use one large office printer across the room. This kept managers at their desks, avoided disruption, and as printers got less and less expensive, we did away with the need for a large, expensive copier/printer that only a certified copier repairman knew how to fix.

Today, efficiencies can be gained through running an agency with proprietary case-management software, which saves time by tracking assignments and staff production from the onset of a case's intake to the final invoicing process. Information is input once and shared with investigators and clients. Reports are uploaded and delivered via e-mail along with the accompanying invoice for services. Invoicing and accounts receivable are all tied together and make managing finances and collecting on outstanding invoices as easy as a mouse click. Today, I manage my office from my car or any remote location where I have an Internet connection. If a client needs a copy of a report or invoice, I can access my Internet-based office application and send it from my smartphone or tablet.

Efficiencies come from many different places, and a business's responsibility is to always look for areas to improve its processes. Everyone is a part of the process, and the manager needs to harness all the feedback and ideas that come from a diverse workforce.

After many years in business, I can say that I have learned one thing, which is that I never stop learning. Learn to be a good listener as ideas will always come to you if you are paying attention.

Recently, I had a graduate student studying applied behavior analysis ask me, "If you could improve any part of your business, what would it be?" I said, "Getting the investigators to spend less time procrastinating about their reports and just getting them in quicker. The sooner I get their investigative reports in the office, the quicker I can bill out their time and get our money." Cash flow is a big part of any business, and your clients need to have their reports before they submit an invoice for payment. Even worse is to have ten investigators turn in nothing one week and then each of them turn in ten reports the following week, making the fluctuation in work unpredictable and overwhelming for a manager. Investigators should have five days to work an assignment and be able to submit their report to the office within two days after working the case. Getting my investigators to routinely turn in five completed reports a week on a steady basis would not only create a constant stream of income but also a predictable work load. No investigative owner should ever assume that the investigator's reports won't have to be reviewed before going to the client. All reports must be reviewed by the owner or manager of the agency, no matter what the skill level of the case investigator may be. After explaining my business in more depth, the grad student asked if I had considered offering incentives to the investigators. I asked why I should have to give an investigator an incentive or reward just for doing his or her job. I explained that I had, in the past, gone this route through a program that rewarded the investigators with the highest bill-outs each week. I also paid a bonus to the investigator who shot the most video each month. I now preferred a tool rather than a stimulus that developed a time-saving procedure. In the past we used dictation machines, outside typists, and voice-recognition software, but they still required a laptop, significant editing, or an unnatural extra act. The grad student asked me if there was any one investigator that seemed to be more productive or turned in work on a more consistent basis, and there was. By interviewing this person, we found that he would text message his notes throughout the day and e-mail them to himself so that most of the report writing work was already done by the end of his day. I personally then tried the same procedure myself, using the notes function on my smartphone. I soon found that having my phone in my hand was more common and natural. We have grown accustomed to having our phones in our hands and it was certainly more natural than holding a dictation recorder or opening my laptop. The process of texting notes was even more convenient than I had expected. I brought my own experience to the next company meeting and encouraged all investigators to text their notes throughout the day. Within one month I saw an increase in the weekly case turn in volume. Investigators were also commenting on the amount of time they were saving in report writing time.

EYE ON THE PI

n order to get into the industry you need to be licensed. Private investigation is a licensed and regulated activity in practically every state.

The states usually have standard applications downloadable online. *Never* take a course online promising you to be a private investigator. Since the licensing of private investigators is a government function, *no online course* or program can get you licensed. Some states, like Georgia and Florida, have *pre-licensing courses* that need to be taken before applying for a license. Many other states have a state exam that must be passed in order to be licensed. All of the state exams I have taken have been very similar in nature. They cover some basic common-sense privacy issues, but mostly focus on state statutes, rules and regulations (which are available through the state's reference material), and licensing guidelines.

No test or pre-licensing course is going to automatically make you a successful PI. It's an occupation that you will grow at over time and one you should expect to put a lot of time into in order to get proficient. While most law enforcement officers will qualify for PI licensure, it does not mean that you'll be fast-tracked to success. It's no secret that only a very small percentage of any police department's staff ever become detectives or has aspirations or interest in being an investigator. Those who are detectives are usually not the individuals we see seeking PI jobs—or at least not the majority. It's usually patrol officers who, for whatever reason, left policing and are now considering PI work. So, many of these individuals have no more or no less skills then the rest of the population seeking PI careers. It's also a concern that less than 1 percent of theft cases nationwide are ever solved, and since these cases are more likely to be in the hands of the first responder, like the patrol officer, they unfortunately get acclimated to not seeing these types of cases get resolved. So we have a person that has been in an environment where not solving cases is the norm. Another factor is that it takes ten times more personnel nationwide to fill all the policing positions, so there are many people who have had police experience but may not have the complimentary skills to work in the private corporate sector as a PI. I have even worked with PI agency owners who are retired federal agents, only to find that the amount of money in the case wasn't worth their time, so they turned down the job, the job took too long to complete, or was just a complete waste of money once it was done. Working in the private sector is very different from working within a government agency, and no one entering the PI business should feel that they are at a disadvantage just because they don't have a law enforcement background.

Employment of private investigators is expected to grow approximately 20 percent over the 2010–'20 decade, much *faster than the average for all occupations.* Increased demand for private detectives and investigators will result from heightened security concerns, increased litigation, and the need to protect confidential information and property of all kinds. We have witnessed the proliferation of criminal activity on the Internet, such as identity theft, spamming, e-mail harassment, and illegal downloading of copyrighted materials. More individuals are investigating care facilities, such as child care providers, hospices, and hospitals. The best opportunities for new jobseekers *will be in entry-level jobs in private investigative agencies.* To track investigators' wages and statistics, refer to the "Occupational Employment and Wages" Code, 33-9021, Private Detectives and Investigators.

With insurance companies employing a large number of investigators who are working independently through an agency, keeping track of the insurance laws in your state can give you an idea of the projected benefit of working in one state over another.

According to the US Bureau of Labor Statistics, the private investigative industry is one of the fastest-growing professions with an average median annual salary of $42,870 ($20.61 per hour). A successful investigator working for himself or herself can make upward of four times this amount. While staff investigators may earn between twenty and thirty dollars an hour, the actual client billing rates are between seventy-five and eighty-five dollars an hour. The toughest part of any business, including the PI business, is longevity. It is crucial for me to provide my clients with information that will be helpful and valuable to them in their business dealings. If they don't see the value in my work, then I won't stay in business. We walk a fine line and have to push the envelope at times to get consistent results. You have to earn your clients' business one case at a time, and no matter how many successful cases you have worked for them in the past, the only case that matters is the one you're currently working on. At the same time, we need to work within the laws governing our activities, respect people's privacy, and work ethically.

Having hired hundreds of investigators, I can tell you that hiring managers usually spend about fifteen seconds looking at your resume. Make sure the resume is no longer than one page and clearly emphasizes your specific interests, like: "working as an insurance defense investigator, conducting surveillance, investigating claims and suspected fraud." Your goal is to get an interview, not tell your whole life story on paper (which won't be read). In our business simple and to-the-point is better. Don't send a copy of your certificates, diplomas, and driver's license or any other documentation unless they specifically ask for something. Make sure that the resume is typed and have an original copy or printed copy handy for the personal interview. Make sure that the telephone number listed on your resume *is not a house phone that you never answer.*

The same goes with the e-mail address; don't use a spouse's e-mail address. Use a telephone number and e-mail address that you check daily, if not hourly. In fact, if you're looking to get into this industry, you should have a smartphone that provides your e-mails instantly and answer or return every call promptly. Most employers will call you to discuss your resume first, and based on the initial phone interview, they will decide if they want to proceed further and meet you in person. Again, keep the conversation professional; you still need to get in front of the hiring manager. The more versatile you are, the more attractive you appear to the employer. You need to realize that you may be needed in another town or that a lot of driving is required. There are also probably fifty people applying for the same job you are, so understand that it's not what the company can do for you, it's what can you do for the company. You need to get used to this concept because this is a performance-oriented business: high pressure, results-oriented, and no complaining or excuses. You will be treated fairly, so don't go into a conversation feeling like they want to take advantage of you.

Being a PI is a lot like being an entrepreneur: you need to be resourceful, independent, and results oriented. Anyone that requires a lot of hand-holding or who doesn't understand what getting results means won't last in the industry. But don't be afraid by all of this tough talk; you'll get the hang of it, but you need to stay focused and work hard. You may find yourself spending more time than originally expected to get something right. But there is nothing wrong with putting in extra time to learn.

Interviewing for a job will be essential, and many companies have assessment tests to calculate how well you know the industry and to determine if you can write. One of the entry-level tests is often watching a video taken by a surveillance investigator. You are then asked to compile a report on what you saw. Sounds simple, right? Well again, you would need to know what you should be paying attention to in order to properly write a report that's reflective of the purpose of the observation or surveillance. For instance, if you are watching a person that allegedly injured his right shoulder in an automobile accident, then your details should focus on the physical activity and how well he conducted this activity or if he was restricted by the injury.

Along with checking your writing ability, a potential employer will also want to gauge your knowledge of the industry. Study their website to learn the nature of their business and the types of cases they work. In Florida and many other states there are also licensing exams that provide you with specific studying material that covers the state's statutes and privacy issues, the use of pretexts, and relative rules and regulations about the industry. Read all the material you can so that you sound informed and prepared.

Today, there are many more excellent investigative agencies than there were when I started out. So the opportunities are far more plentiful than thirty years ago, and this is only expected to increase. Most of the more successful companies will be nationwide to service the largest nationwide companies.

Another factor that will lead to the increase of needed professional PIs will be new legislation. Many states have considered enacting civil actions against scammers, which would mean more investigative work for the PI. The actions would impose large civil fines, and the fraudsters would pay far beyond the insurance money they stole. Civil actions are especially useful in dismantling the big fraudsters that traffic in staged crashes, healthcare schemes, and other lucrative big-dollar fraud enterprises.

For those of you that do take that job as a PI, remember that you are only as good as your last case, and you are evaluated not by what you think you know but what you deliver. And while some business owners like to say "everyone can be replaced," if you find yourself in a position of responsibility over others, learn to show your appreciation and empower your staff to make their own decisions. Finally, I know I'm not the first person to say this, but it may be the first time you have heard it, so it's worth repeating: clients are hard to come by, and "it costs more money to look for new clients than it does to keep the ones you have satisfied." So don't underestimate the importance that your interaction with them makes and always provide excellent customer service!

The goal of this book was to provide information and insight about the modern-day Private Investigator. Many students with an interest in Criminal Justice and Investigations should know that there is a growing industry of professional private investigators that have had very successful careers in the industry. By considering this additional career option, the job seeking student opens up their job search to another possible sixty thousand positions. The more qualified people we have entering the field, the stronger we will make our industry.

THE AUTHOR

John Bilyk started his career as a staff investigator joining a small investigations firm. He worked to grow one of the largest investigative firms in the country before moving on to start his own nationwide agency. He was licensed and practiced as a PI in twelve states throughout the United States and the Commonwealth of Puerto Rico. As a director and board member, he organized the first associate's degree program in Florida for private investigations through the Institute of Specialized Training and Management (ISTM, later purchased by City College). In 1995, he became a Certified Fraud Examiner and considered an expert in insurance claims investigations. As a lifelong private investigator, he is devoted to the private investigations industry, teaching, writing, and training. He has trained hundreds of investigators who have made private investigations their career.

Are you next?

www.ingramcontent.com/pod-product-compliance
Lightning Source LLC
Chambersburg PA
CBHW072008040426
42447CB00009B/1544